CLARITY
focusing on what matters

weekly readings for
next-level leadership

SHANDEL SLATEN, MCC

Visit www.truelifecoaching.com.

ISBN-10: 0-9708587-8-7
ISBN-13: 978-0-9708587-8-8

Printed in the United States of America

dedication

For my mom, Sandy, a woman of great clarity, especially when it came to the character she instilled in her children. Mom, the focus you gave to molding me into a leader has inspired countless others to do the same.

CONTENTS

SETTING THE STAGE .... *vii*

YOU NEED TO READ THIS .... *ix*

YOU NEED TO READ THIS, TOO .... *xiii*

WEEK 1: CHARACTER	ARE YOU A JELLYFISH OR AN EAGLE?	2
WEEK 2: TIME	F.O.C.U.S. ON WHAT MATTERS	4
WEEK 3: PURPOSE	LEADERSHIP IS A CALLING	6
WEEK 4: TIME	IT'S SIMPLE -- IT'S JUST NOT EASY	8
WEEK 5: VALUES	THE POWER OF VALUES	10
WEEK 6: CHARACTER	S.T.O.P. YOUR INNER CRITIC	12
WEEK 7: VALUES	PERSPECTIVE EQUALS PATIENCE	14
WEEK 8: COMMUNICATION	KEEPING SHORT ACCOUNTS	16
WEEK 9: CHARACTER	THE POWER OF SELF-ACCEPTANCE	18
WEEK 10: TRUST	ANTI-TRUST LAWS	20
WEEK 11: CHARACTER	DO YOU HAVE WHAT IT TAKES?	22
WEEK 12: PURPOSE	WHEN I GROW UP I WANT TO BE SIGNIFICANT	24
WEEK 13: CHARACTER	WAKE UP, EINSTEIN	26
WEEK 14: COMMUNICATION	COMMUNICATION THEORY 101	28
WEEK 15: VALUES	AVOIDING THE BUMP IN THE ROAD	30
WEEK 16: TIME	HASTE MAKES WASTE	32
WEEK 17: CHARACTER	REACHING THE TOP TOGETHER	34
WEEK 18: CHARACTER	THE MESSAGE OF ANGER	36
WEEK 19: PURPOSE	A LIFE OF INTEGRITY	38
WEEK 20: CHARACTER	THE MEEK AND WILD	40
WEEK 21: TIME	JUMPING OFF THE HAMSTER WHEEL	42
WEEK 22: COMMUNICATION	MISCOMMUNICATION AND OTHER RELATIONAL HAZARDS	44

WEEK 23: VALUES HOW DO YOU SPELL RELIEF? 46

WEEK 24: CHARACTER/COURAGE REAL RISK IN RELATIONSHIP 48

WEEK 25: VALUES EXPOSING OUR FOUNDATIONS 50

WEEK 26: CHARACTER DON'T KILL YOUR CURIOSITY 52

WEEK 27: COMMUNICATION CAN YOU WIN AT DEFENSE? 54

WEEK 28: PURPOSE BE WHO YOU ARE... 56

WEEK 29: CHARACTER KEEPING BUSY TO AVOID
RESPONSIBILITY... 58

WEEK 30: TRUST GROWING TRUST 60

WEEK 31: CHARACTER/COURAGE BALANCED BODY BUILDING 62

WEEK 32: CHARACTER/COURAGE PREPARING FOR SUCCESS........................... 64

WEEK 33: CHARACTER/COURAGE REDEFINING F.E.A.R. 66

WEEK 34: COMMUNICATION THE SILENT KILLER 68

WEEK 35: VALUES WHAT IS YOUR PERSONAL
OPERATING SYSTEM? 70

WEEK 36: TIME NAVIGATING THROUGH STRESS 72

WEEK 37: CHARACTER SADDLE UP ANYWAY 74

WEEK 38: VALUES GIVERS OR TAKERS 76

WEEK 39: CHARACTER/COURAGE GUARANTEED NOT TO FAIL 78

WEEK 40: COMMUNICATION HIDING BEHIND BUSYNESS 80

WEEK 41: VALUES TO ERR IS HUMAN, TO FORGIVE
IS GOOD BUSINESS.. 82

WEEK 42: TRUST TRUST STARTS WITH YOU 84

WEEK 43: COMMUNICATION AVOIDING THE BEACH BALL 86

WEEK 44: PURPOSE BUILDING A LEGACY NOW........................... 88

WEEK 45: CHARACTER CHARACTER IN SMALL MOMENTS.............. 90

WEEK 46: PURPOSE LIVING THE ONLY DAY YOU HAVE.............. 92

WEEK 47: TIME PUSHING YOUR LIMITS 94

WEEK 48: TRUST TRUST YOUR GUT 96

WEEK 49: CHARACTER/COURAGE CHOOSING TO GO FORWARD 98

WEEK 50: VALUES DISCOVERING THE WHY FACTOR 100

WEEK 51: CHARACTER/COURAGE YOU CAN GO HIGHER.................................102

WEEK 52: PURPOSE WHAT IS YOUR DREAM? 104

ABOUT SHANDEL SLATEN, MCC 107

ABOUT TRUE LIFE COACHING...107

SETTING THE STAGE

Clarity: Focusing on What Matters is for people who want to take their own life to the next level and lead others effectively.

My passion is helping leaders lead well. After having worked with leaders of all stripes, backgrounds, and ages, I firmly believe that leadership is about what you do for others, the influence you have, and the opportunity to serve as many people as you can along the way. I want this book to provide the tools you need to achieve clarity in your own life and, more importantly, to pass that clarity along to others in your sphere of influence so that you can maximize your effectiveness as a leader.

Regardless of whether you intend to or not, you influence the people you interact with, for better or worse, every single day. The question is: how are you currently making an impact: for better, or worse? My hope is that the principles laid out in *Clarity* will help you make a positive impact.

This journey towards clarity can begin as soon as you're ready to open your heart and mind to embrace hope, focus, and purpose. In short, this journey takes courage! I have no doubt that it will be an adventure, and I want to share it with you. Connect with me on our True Life blog (www.truelifecoaching.com), Facebook, and Twitter for encouragement, tips, and tools along the way.

Get clear and get going!

Shandel Slaten
March 2011

YOU NEED TO READ THIS

As leaders, we are always moving toward something. When it is a powerful vision that has purpose and meaning, we move quickly. However, when that vision gets blocked — whether by the "how," the "why" or the "who" — productivity, energy, and fulfillment wane as fear and insecurity escalate. When this persists, and we continue down an unfocused, unfulfilled path, we will hit a wall that ricochets us into a pit of despair.

> "People cannot climb beyond the limitations of their character."
> — John C Maxwell

What makes us lose sight of our most important goals? Why is it so easy to wander away from our plan? How do we get derailed so quickly? Generally, it is because we are not being truthful with ourselves. In my experience, it usually involves challenges in one or more of these areas: *character, communication, purpose, time management, trust, and values.* When you lose focus in any one of these areas, you can guarantee your key relationships from the bedroom to the corner office are going to suffer.

You are either gaining or losing influence and trust as leaders. This book provides small steps that will leverage your efforts and help you improve your level of operational influence, productivity and purpose.

The Path to Clarity

If you're feeling unclear about your goals right now, if there's something blocking your vision, this 52-week journey will help you gain the focus you need to move your forward.

As you work through each week's reading and response, you'll find insight that can illuminate your path to clarity. Leaders must be trained in areas of head and heart, people and task, and personality and process. The stories and examples in each lesson will appeal to a change of heart so that, when connected with the truth of the issue, your brain will execute the behavioral change.

The Weekly Review: Take the Challenge

WHEN I WAS AROUND EIGHT YEARS OLD, MY DAD PARAPHRASED A quote from Albert Einstein in his own mountain-raised manner. "Sis, you'll keep gettin' what'cher gettin' if you keep doin' what'cher doin'."

I would add my two cents to that today: if you don't change your perspective, challenge your limiting beliefs, and identify your blind spots, you will keep trying to change on the outside what can only be changed from the inside. And you'll end up frustrated.

Clarity comes to the humble. To the teachable person who is courageous enough to challenge their beliefs and to stretch themselves every year, week by week, day by day, moment by moment.

When I read David Allen's book, *Getting Things Done: The Art of*

HERE ARE THE BASIC STEPS TO DAVID ALLEN'S WEEKLY REVIEW:

- Pull out all loose papers, receipts, Post-Its, etc., and put in your inbox.
- Process your inbox.
- Process your notes.
- Review previous and upcoming calendar data to trigger next actions.
- Mind-dump: empty your head of everything not already in the system. Process it as you would your inbox.
- Review next-action lists, project lists, waiting-on list, and someday/maybe list.
- Review your goals.

Stress-Free Productivity (Penguin, 2002), I was inspired by his idea of the Weekly Review. I realized how helpful it would be to start your week off with a personal leadership challenge to complement the usual list of activities and priorities. If we can develop the habit of intentionally doing one thing per week to strengthen our character and relationships, what transformed people we would be in one year's time. Are you ready for that challenge?

The clear journey towards *Next-Level Leadership* starts with reading a weekly entry and answering the following questions:

- What is my leadership intention this week?
- How I will benefit from this shift?
- What might hinder my success?
- What action must I take in response?
- What am I learning about myself?
- What did I do this week that I am proud of?

Next, let's take a look at these questions in greater detail.

YOU NEED TO READ THIS, TOO

FLIPPING THROUGH *CLARITY* WON'T HELP YOU REACH A NEW LEVEL of confidence unless you interact with the material in a personal and practical way. That's why I've included six questions at the end of each weekly reading.

I recommend sitting down with *Clarity* at the same time every week, perhaps on Sunday evening as you prepare for the coming week. After each reading, take a moment to reflect and challenge yourself. Decide on an action to take the following week, and hold yourself accountable!

Let's look at each question. An example is supplied to get you started.

What Is My Leadership Intention This Week?

THE INTENTION MAY COME FROM THE READING, OR FROM ANOTHER area in your life urgently needing attention. Make sure it is realistic and attainable within one week. Envision it. Your mind needs a picture of where you want to go — and the more detailed the better. Then state your intention as a positive statement so that your mind can get you there.

Example: *I will listen to Bobby with my full attention 3x this week.* (In other words, "I will stop checking my phone and Facebook while my son is talking to me.")

How I Will Benefit from This Shift?

YOUR INTENTION — THE ACTION YOU'RE GOING TO TAKE — IS A shift. But is it a "should do" or a "want to do"? Here is where you need to coach yourself. We don't do things we *should* do; we do things we *want* to do and which benefit us. So, how will your weekly intention benefit you?

Example: *I want my son to know he is valuable to me, and I don't want that guilty knot in my gut.*

What Might Hinder My Success?

HERE YOU MUST BE HONEST ABOUT WHAT IS REALLY GOING ON IN your life. Face the truth about what is standing in the way of your intention. Count the cost. What will get in the way? What will hinder your success? If you correctly address the hindrance you can take steps to remove the block.

Example: *The contract negotiations should be finalized this week. I will be anxious until they are.*

What Action Must I Take in Response?

THIS IS WHERE YOU GET SPECIFIC ABOUT HOW YOU ARE GOING TO achieve your goal. Speak truth to yourself and be courageous enough to deal with the hindrance so that you can make your intention a realistic part of your day-to-day life.

Example: *My son is more important than the contract negotiation, so I can carve out time to prioritize him first, giving him my full attention and then explain at other times why I am distracted.*

What Am I Learning about Myself?

THIS IS A GREAT PLACE TO THINK ABOUT THE LEGACY YOU ARE leaving. A place to document the ups and downs of the journey. Be honest, so that next year you are able to reflect quickly on your progress and lessons learned.

Example: *I am learning that I set high standards for myself at the price of my family. I would rather please my manager than please my son. I am grateful to see it now so I can change it now.*

What Did I Do This Week that I Am Proud Of?

THIS IS A PLACE TO REFLECT ON THE PREVIOUS WEEK'S INTENTION OR record other victories of your week. Leaders are notorious for not celebrating their wins. As you force yourself to reflect on your wins, you will be able to celebrate and look for wins in others.

Example (this would be recorded on the following week's page): *I am proud that I spent two full nights unplugged and focused on my son. The look in his eyes told me all I needed to know. When we lost the chance for a third night because of the contract negotiations, my son not only understood but celebrated with me. I feel grateful.*

What follows are 52 readings, one for each week of the year. Remember, they're tagged with one of six dominate themes important to clarity: character, communication, purpose, time, trust, and values. Some may feel similar in content, but it's intentional — repetition drives home the crucial concepts you need to strengthen your *Next-Level Leadership* skills.

Make a commitment to reading once a week, whether sequentially or in whatever order you like. If not now, when?

CLARITY

Focusing on What Matters

Weekly Readings for

Next-Level Leadership

ARE YOU A JELLYFISH OR AN EAGLE?

HAVE YOU EVER BEEN FRUSTRATED BY PEOPLE WHOSE LIVES SEEM SO smooth and easy, while you are working diligently only to encounter trial after trial?

When I was fresh out of college, I posed that question to my wise mentor. Answering my jealousy over the easy life of my peers, he explained that there are two types of people: jellyfish and eagles. Building upon his words, I have used this analogy throughout the years to encourage greatness in others.

"Imagine that you have no limitations on what you can be, have or do. If you were completely free to choose, what changes would you make in your life? Deal honestly and objectively with yourself; intellectual honesty and personal courage are the hallmarks of great character."

— *Brian Tracy*

Consider the jellyfish. Sure, it gets blown and tossed by the tide of the sea, but basically it just floats along. It lives on what comes its way. There's not too much conflict, and no need for adventure. Just enough movement to stay with the current until it dies.

There may be a few exceptional jellyfish that stand out, but a jellyfish is a jellyfish — content blobs existing in the sea. For a jellyfish, there is nothing wrong with that. Nothing else is expected of a jellyfish.

Now consider the eagle. Food doesn't just come bobbing by for the eagle — it has to go get it. Have you ever watched how many times an eagle will dive for its dinner? Relentless! For goodness sakes, on the first day of flight school, the baby eagle gets dropped out of the nest!

While they have an incredible view from the top of the world, they often perch alone because of their choice for higher living. The trials and difficulties of the eagle are what breed the character we admire: courage, vigor, and freedom. Nothing is abnormal about the challenging adventure they live — that's an eagle's life. Nothing less should be expected.

Unlike the animal kingdom, humans have a choice in how they want to live and who they want to be. You choose your attitude and your behavior. It doesn't matter if jellyfish parents raised you; you can learn to be an eagle. I've seen organizations with jellyfish CEOs and eagle janitors. It's not your position; it's your attitude.

The challenge is when you naively see yourself soaring like an eagle, but you are blind to your jellyfish lifestyle. Anyone can be an eagle, but you must commit to pay the personal cost of higher living and consistent integrity. Choose today to find higher ground and learn the way of an eagle.

YOUR WEEKLY RESPONSE

What is my leadership intention this week? _____
_____
_____

How I will benefit from this shift? _____
_____
_____

What might hinder my success? _____
_____
_____

What action must I take in response? _____
_____
_____

What am I learning about myself? _____
_____
_____

What did I do this week that I am proud of? _____
_____
_____

F.O.C.U.S. ON WHAT MATTERS

I LOVE ACRONYMS. THEY HELP US REMEMBER KEY THOUGHTS. TODAY I want you to F.O.C.U.S. on a few important things.

First things first! Prioritize your core values first. Seriously, what matters most to you? Honor it! Put your money, time, and energy where your mouth is and not what "you wish for." Focus on your priorities and set boundaries around what steals time, energy, and money from the people and things you value most. This is not optional if you want to live an intentional life.

Others. How can you serve others versus seek to be served? Leadership is always about serving those who serve you. Reflect on what would you do if the important others were not in your life tomorrow. Let them know today how important they are to you. If not now, when?

> "What matters is where you want to go. Focus in the right direction!"
>
> — Donald Trump

Celebrate what has gone right. We do not celebrate enough so take a moment to use your words and celebrate! Then use what has worked well to simplify your life even more. It is in the time of celebrating we are able to clearly see people's talents and we can use that to focus on the strengths of both yourself and others.

Uphold your integrity; keep your promises. Make it your ambition to *under-promise* and *over-deliver*. Might I add, apply this especially to your kids, if you have them, or work with them. It absolutely makes me sick when I see adults have to break even a small promise to wide-eyed expectant children. Your integrity is tested more with your words and promises than anywhere else. Uphold your integrity keep: your promises.

Simplify everything. What can you say no to, so that you can say yes to what matters? What boundaries do you need to set so that you are honoring your values? What beliefs no longer serve you? What junk in your house, office, car, files, etc., needs to be thrown out to bring clarity?

Focusing on what matters can do wonders for your clarity as a professional, as a family member, as a parent, as a friend. Next step is to get support from your coach, partner, spouse or peer group to keep that focus!

YOUR WEEKLY RESPONSE

What is my leadership intention this week? _____
_____
_____

How I will benefit from this shift? _____
_____
_____

What might hinder my success? _____
_____
_____

What action must I take in response? _____
_____
_____

What am I learning about myself? _____
_____
_____

What did I do this week that I am proud of? _____
_____
_____

LEADERSHIP IS A CALLING

WHEN I WAS 19 AND IN MY SECOND YEAR OF COLLEGE, I GOT A surprise call to lead a group of high school students. It required me to move away from my rockin' college experience. I would have to report to a board. I was way too young and inexperienced, and I resisted at first. The whole thing was a huge risk and a complete unknown.

But just as the phone rang unexpectedly, so my heart was moved unexpectedly toward these kids. I will never regret saying yes. More important than the leadership role I played, I learned the fulfillment of saying yes when the decision is a matter of calling versus the next logical career move. I found purpose in the work, rather than working for some other vague purpose.

> *"Before you are a leader, success is all about growing yourself. When you become a leader, success is all about growing others."*
>
> — Jack Welch

Ten years later, on August 17, 2000, I attended the NYC Entrepreneurs Organization University. One of the workshops was on why as entrepreneurs we needed a coach. Right there, at 2 pm in Times Square, I knew I was supposed to be a coach. I heard another call. True Life Coaching was born.

What is your calling? I want you to slow down for five minutes, get real quiet and ask yourself that question. Usually the answer is right under your nose.

I believe that leadership is a calling, not a job. It's a privilege to lead, not a right or obligation. We aren't just executives with people underneath us on an org chart who are basically a means to an end. If you're like that, your business books may tell you you're supposed to care, but truth be told your direct reports are a nuisance. That is a job. Merely a job, even if you're the business owner, the director, a manager or the CEO.

If you have people for whom you are responsible, then, like it or not, you are a leader, and those people need you to care, truly care, for them. They are your calling. (That includes the little ones at home.)

It's noble and big, but is not difficult. It's simple, actually; it's just not easy.

Seriously, life is too short to just keep working at a job. Answer the call because you don't know how long the call will last.

YOUR WEEKLY RESPONSE

What is my leadership intention this week? _____
_____
_____

How I will benefit from this shift? _____
_____
_____

What might hinder my success? _____
_____
_____

What action must I take in response? _____
_____
_____

What am I learning about myself? _____
_____
_____

What did I do this week that I am proud of? _____
_____
_____

WEEK 4: TIME

IT'S SIMPLE — IT'S JUST NOT EASY

RECENTLY, I ASKED A CLIENT WHO WAS JUGGLING A LIFE WITH A million moving parts what his payoff was. His answer was insightful. "I guess because not many people can handle the level of complexity I face daily." Yep, our ego is usually the villain in our unfulfilled busy life.

My next question was what was the *cost* for this lifestyle? His response was brilliant: Busy-ness that prevents him from working toward the things that matter most to him and his long-term vision.

Yes, he was getting his emotional need of accomplishment fulfilled. But at an expensive long-term cost... *his life*!

Is your life complicated? Would you like to work smarter, rather than harder, toward what really matters? The first step is to simplify.

"Sometimes the questions are complicated and the answers are simple."

— *Dr. Seuss*

When I began working with my client on this issue, it wasn't long that I heard him say, "Hey, this simplifying is hard."

Yes! It is! Especially at first.

Consider the lack of productivity and the low morale at your workplace. What's the simple answer? Invest in the lives of your people, empower and equip the team, and let go of controlling every detail (in other words, trust!). Simple answer. Oh, but that is not easy, is it?

Instead what do we do? We complicate our processes, procedures, systems, and emails — so we don't have to deal with humans. We tell ourselves that all this nonsense helps mitigate the overwhelming demands we face.

It's okay to LOL at yourself. I do!

What if you could simplify everything? More importantly, what if you could simplify everything for the team you lead, and be able to trust that what needs to get done will get done? What if you did not get your worth from how "busy" and complex your life is, and instead made the choice to intentionally delete everything that does not align with your values?

This is what would happen: You would probably be more fulfilled, more focused, and a heck of a lot more fun to be around!

Values help you make better decisions faster. Unfortunately, they are the first thing we compromise in a complicated life!

How complicated is your life? Is it worth it? What can you simplify today and what is the reward for you and those you lead? Those you love? Those who matter most?

YOUR WEEKLY RESPONSE

What is my leadership intention this week? _____
_____
_____

How I will benefit from this shift? _____
_____
_____

What might hinder my success? _____
_____
_____

What action must I take in response? _____
_____
_____

What am I learning about myself? _____
_____
_____

What did I do this week that I am proud of? _____
_____
_____

THE POWER OF VALUES

IMAGINE YOU HAVE JUST ENOUGH TIME FOR LUNCH TO POP INTO A Taco Del Mar on the way to your meeting. What to order? Umm, that build-your-own burrito with the rice and beans looks yummy. But then again, you're on a diet.

Those refried beans look so good... hey you committed to eat healthier food, and the self-talk rages. You could have the taco salad. It doesn't look too boring, if they top it with sour cream ... Someone coughs and you realize you're holding up the line. Shoot, it's hard to decide...

"Be proactive. Ask yourself, 'Are my actions based on self-chosen values or on my moods, feelings and circumstances?'"
— Stephen Covey

It doesn't need to be. If you had already defined and established health as one of your top three values, you could walk into any fast-food restaurant (well, most of them) and place your order in 5 seconds.

This is a silly example, but knowing your core values allows you to stop reacting, and start responding to life. They empower you to live in full integrity bringing your words, beliefs, and actions into alignment.

Just like every company, every person has core values that make up who we are, what we want, and how we live. The problem is most of us have not taken the time and energy to discover and label what our top values are. That's a shame, because if you are not living by your own values, you're living by someone else's.

Think of your values as the rudder that guides your life. They are at the core of who you are. When we are living in integrity, values are what we are naturally inclined to, drawn to, or eager to do, without "effort." In well-defined companies, values are the standards by which management, hires, fires, rewards, disciplines, and promotes within — in short the why we do what we do.

Why are values so important? Because honoring your values is the quickest route to living a fulfilled life. Ironically, values are easily veiled by needs, stress, addictions, unresolved matters, "should's," "have-tos" and the things that drain us. Even the things that bring us moments of satisfaction and surface happiness can squeeze out our values at times.

Clarified values help you hold to the standards you have set for yourself. They also help you establish the boundaries you need when it comes to others' behavior. With that roadmap, you can reach your goals, and get rid of the goals that aren't really yours. Like refried beans with cheese and sour cream.

YOUR WEEKLY RESPONSE

What is my leadership intention this week? _____
_____
_____

How I will benefit from this shift? _____
_____
_____

What might hinder my success? _____
_____
_____

What action must I take in response? _____
_____
_____

What am I learning about myself? _____
_____
_____

What did I do this week that I am proud of? _____
_____
_____

S.T.O.P. YOUR INNER CRITIC

IS YOUR LEADERSHIP STYLE MARKED BY JOY OR JUDGMENT? HAVE YOU lost your happiness and creativity? If so, you may want to take a moment and evaluate if you are being too critical. You may have fleeting moments of feeling happy or even a night of laughter, but are they short-lived because that inner critic starts chattering again?

Joy and criticism cannot co-exist. When you choose to be judgmental and criticize, you turn in your joy card!

Secure and confident people have a radiant, contagious peace and calmness that allows them to find joy in the journey without a constant need to judge others for their own sense of self.

Insecure people, on the other hand, judge others so that they can find a moment of relief from their inner critic. Nothing is ever good enough. Some people even view their relentless "never-good-enough" attitude as their reason for success. That is a lie.

I believe you can obtain healthy contentment and joy that actually creates more energy and vision to lead forward. Joy energizes a purpose and vision that pulls you forward into what you were created to be and do. In contrast, guilt drags you along with a ball and chain, telling you you're still not quite good enough yet.

"If you think you can, or you think you can't, you're right."
— *Henry Ford*

When you start talking or thinking in a judgmental way, remember to S.T.O.P.!

Here are four quick tips to S.T.O.P. the negative critic and become a joy giver and receiver:

S: Separate your expectations and personal preference to see reality and creativity.

T: Thankful — It's hard to be critical and thankful at the same time. Be grateful!

O: Overlook or confront? If you are not going to confront something, then overlook it. If you can't overlook it, then confront it! Do not allow yourself another choice.

P: Perspective — Is what you are all worked up about worth giving up joy for?

I invite you to participate in an honest evaluation of your leadership style that starts with your inner person. The negative inner critic does not provide a good return on your energy. It makes you look small and insecure. You have so much to offer. Don't settle!

Stop justifying a cynical, critical spirit. Swap it with joy.

Hold on to your joy card!

YOUR WEEKLY RESPONSE

What is my leadership intention this week? _____
_____
_____

How I will benefit from this shift? _____
_____
_____

What might hinder my success? _____
_____
_____

What action must I take in response? _____
_____
_____

What am I learning about myself? _____
_____
_____

What did I do this week that I am proud of? _____
_____
_____

PERSPECTIVE EQUALS PATIENCE

HAVE YOU EVER EXPERIENCED YOURSELF IN THE MIDDLE OF A LIFE lesson?

I did once, in front of the UC San Francisco hospital. We were on a tight schedule, trying to navigate the mess of those tiny uphill streets and find parking. My three-month-old nephew, scheduled for a three-hour kidney surgery the next morning, was crying in his car seat. A vehicle had stopped right in traffic lane of the parking garage, causing a huge backup.

"A loving person lives in a loving world. A hostile person lives in a hostile world. Everyone you meet is your mirror."

— Ken Keyes

I'm not a patient person. But unexpectedly, I was in full awareness of a sense of patience as I looked out the window to see the cause of the backup. A boy emerged from the passenger side and opened the door for an elderly woman, perhaps his grandmother. I recognized the dialysis branding on the bag she was carrying, and I flashed to the days I spent with my dad during his dialysis treatments.

As their car moved on, I noticed that none of the drivers seemed upset. There was compassion and understanding in the air. I realized what was going on and immediately applied it to a life lesson.

When we have context, we have patience. When we have information, we have understanding. When we have clarity and see pain, we have compassion. When we get inside people's world, we have perspective. When we have all of that, we have grace, because we are no longer judging and condemning from our own paradigm. In a moment, our paradigm has broadened and shifted.

When we enter into the other person's world, we stop demanding he or she fit into ours. We slow down enough to be grateful for our own good fortune and stop judging others for their assumed inadequacies.

A leader gets results through people. People are wounded. We still need to get results. Results can be hindered because our people are wounded, and if we would deal with the wound or help them deal with it — we would get better, faster results.

Patience is not a natural gift of a leader, it is a learned one. The more that you broaden your awareness, understanding, and compassion, the better results you will get out of your people. (It's called emotional intelligence, by the way.)

Be patient. You'll get your results.

YOUR WEEKLY RESPONSE

What is my leadership intention this week? _____
_____
_____

How I will benefit from this shift? _____
_____
_____

What might hinder my success? _____
_____
_____

What action must I take in response? _____
_____
_____

What am I learning about myself? _____
_____
_____

What did I do this week that I am proud of? _____
_____
_____

KEEPING SHORT ACCOUNTS

IT'S IMPOSSIBLE TO HIDE THE FACT THAT THE GARBAGE IS OVERDUE for its trip to the dumpster, isn't it? You can always tell when you forget to empty the trash. Sniff sniff. What's that odor? Oh...

Your waste management may not be as bad as New York City's famous 17-day sanitation strike a few decades ago, but the garbage can is one area of life you want to keep empty on a regular basis.

Verbal garbage is too.

Think of your angry, mean, or hurtful words like the office trash. As long as the rubbish is dealt with on a daily basis, no one makes an issue about it. If it's neglected, though, it begins to stink up the entire business or the whole house. Now everyone is affected.

"Everybody thinks of changing humanity, but nobody thinks of changing himself."

— Leo Tolstoy

When you do not admit fault and don't ask for forgiveness; when you assume time will atone for your inconsiderate words; when you put a lid on the problem and hide it in the corner, you stink things up. Ironically, you sometimes even have the gall to ask, "What smells bad?"

My friend, if you are not taking responsibility for your words and the effect they have on other people, you could be living in a landfill of your own verbal trash. You must keep your accounts short.

Here's what I mean by keeping accounts short. Examine your life daily. Have you spoken any words that have broken a colleague's stride, words that have brought employees down rather than built them up? If you say something hurtful or insensitive and recognize that it causes pain (even if you don't know why anyone could take it that way), go back to the person with a sincere desire to clean up the mess.

For some reason, we think that if we withdraw and ignore it long enough, the offense will go away and its harmful effect will disappear. Oftentimes this thought process is reinforced when our spouse, friend, or co-worker is more concerned about the relationship than their hurt feelings. Thus, they take the "high road," and we do not have to take responsibility for our harmful words or actions.

Apologize for causing a stink!

Then smile as you put the new liner in the trash can, creating a sweet-smelling environment — knowing you'll need to do it again tomorrow.

But for today you've got a clean slate.

YOUR WEEKLY RESPONSE

What is my leadership intention this week? _____
_____
_____

How I will benefit from this shift? _____
_____
_____

What might hinder my success? _____
_____
_____

What action must I take in response? _____
_____
_____

What am I learning about myself? _____
_____
_____

What did I do this week that I am proud of? _____
_____
_____

THE POWER OF SELF-ACCEPTANCE

I LOVE MY DAD'S GREAT SENSE OF HUMOR. MORE THAN TWENTY years ago he received a pancreas-kidney transplant, and must take medication daily to prevent his body from rejecting his new organs. Whenever I need to apologize to him, he jokes, "It's okay, I took my anti-rejection meds."

We laugh, but it gets me thinking. I need some! Emotional rejection is at the root of nearly every issue in my life and my clients' lives. Is it in yours, too?

"You can preach a better sermon with your life than with your lips."
— Oliver Goldsmith

Every person, even the most powerful executive in your industry, longs to be accepted just as they are, without fear of losing love because they are not "good enough." There is an unconscious need to prove something — to someone.

In the business world, it can lead to an ugly cycle. As employers or managers, we load our plates with ever expanding big goals, driven by the adrenaline of "we can do this." Then we turn to our people, who haven't even accomplished the first set of goals, to get cracking on a new set of initiatives. While getting frustrated that nothing ever gets done!

The employee feels pressure to meet the demands of the manager who works 12-hour days and creates volumes of work requiring them to work 12 hours a day to keep up. Fear of rejection — fear of losing their jobs — keeps them from standing up for themselves and saying, "Hey, this project deadline is not realistic." So they sabotage deadlines in a passive-aggressive stew, burn out, or quit.

To truly be a great leader, we need to go under the microscope and see where rejection is deterring our greatest leadership potential. We must take proactive action to remove the threat from our lives so we can live and lead the way we long to do so — from acceptance and appreciation of one's true self, not the mask we want everyone else to adore and worship.

What's your anti-rejection drug? Self-acceptance. Humility. Grace.

Swallow it completely, and regularly! Your greatest legacy is what you do for others and yet that has to start with how you view yourself. I challenge you to be the best you can be, accept your unique strengths and limits, so that in turn you can accept others. In celebrating their uniqueness, you are celebrating your own!

YOUR WEEKLY RESPONSE

What is my leadership intention this week? _____
_____
_____

How I will benefit from this shift? _____
_____
_____

What might hinder my success? _____
_____
_____

What action must I take in response? _____
_____
_____

What am I learning about myself? _____
_____
_____

What did I do this week that I am proud of? _____
_____
_____

ANTI-TRUST LAWS

WHEN I WAS ABOUT 10, MY MOM TAUGHT ME AN IMPORTANT LESSON.

"Shandel," Mom said, "I will trust you until the day you break my trust. After that I will absolutely love you and forgive you, but it will be impossible to trust you at the same level I fully trust you at today."

She gave this example: If I said I was going to Sears and went to a movie instead, she would always wonder if, the next time I said I was going to Sears, I was lying.

In my work I encounter on a daily basis what I think is the worst virus in organizations today: A lack of trust.

"It's not hard to make decisions when you know what your values are."

— Roy Disney

Say everyone has been doing their best but business grew so fast it is out of control and stress levels have been high for so long that everyone is burned out and fighting in their passive-aggressive, politically-correct way. The first sign that trust is eroding is a biggie: lack of communication.

If you do not recognize there has been a breakdown of communication, you will soon see its evidence: high turnover, disgruntled attitudes, an apathetic work environment. All the while, your goals aren't being reached, or worse yet, they're being reached at too high of an emotional cost.

Where does leadership fit in? Leaders are usually the last to know there is a breakdown of trust. It can really take them off guard.

Why? First, leaders have control, thus they can be deceived that all is well. Second, when trust erodes, people stop talking while they disengage. Leaders can mistake apathetic acquiescence as agreeable compliance. Third, some leaders may be so far out ahead strategizing at 30,000 feet that they are not connected to the reality at ground level. Thus when a problem is brought up, the leader jumps to action before seeking the true source of the problem — furthering the lack of trust in leadership.

What's the anti-virus solution?

You can regain trust — but it takes a deliberate commitment, hard work, lots of proven time, and a little divine intervention. The key is team building. But remember, taking no action to eradicate this virus is a deliberate choice.

Take action today!

_____

YOUR WEEKLY RESPONSE

What is my leadership intention this week? _____
_____
_____

How I will benefit from this shift? _____
_____
_____

What might hinder my success? _____
_____
_____

What action must I take in response? _____
_____
_____

What am I learning about myself? _____
_____
_____

What did I do this week that I am proud of? _____
_____
_____

DO YOU HAVE WHAT IT TAKES?

Do I have what it takes?

Does this question haunt you? I'd say most leaders wrestle with it, no matter how successful they are.

For some high achievers, not having an answer troubles them in the quiet moments of their soul. Thus, they avoid quiet moments, and deny their soul. Instead, they live a chaotic life to prove to the world, *Yes! I do have what it takes! Look at my busy schedule, my buzzing phone, my overflowing inbox. Of course I have what it takes!*

Driven behavior and false bravado reinforce the lie that that you must prove your success to be of worth.

You must first answer a different question: *Do I know what it takes?*

> "Success is getting what you want; happiness is wanting what you get."
>
> — Dale Carnegie

You are chasing someone else's definition of success, unless you have established your own. So how do *you* define success? What is your purpose? What are your values?

For example, I can't tell you the number of our clients who are unconsciously driven to gain the approval of a family member, teacher, or coach. Here's the problem. The authority they are trying to impress is oblivious, or is proud of them already, or has given up whatever they said 20 years ago — or is dead!

You'll never get what you need from another human. Your sense of success must come from where you put your hope, your value, your identity. That is your choice and that is your responsibility. You decide.

Do I want what it takes and why?

That's the real question that separates you from the rest. Do you want to be the best *you*?

You may say no because the rat race is all you have ever known. If you take the dare to change, perhaps you fear your motivation will be lost; you'll be lost.

What is the answer? Clarity. Passion. Anger as a driving force is negative and draining. It can be replaced with a deep sense of purpose and clear definition of your worth and success.

Last question: *What is standing in your way?*

Identify what is hindering you from wanting to pursue that deeper sense of self. Then take the first step.

You have a specific reason you were put on Earth at this time in history and the world is waiting for you to live your true self.

You do indeed have what it takes.

YOUR WEEKLY RESPONSE

What is my leadership intention this week? _____
_____
_____

How I will benefit from this shift? _____
_____
_____

What might hinder my success? _____
_____
_____

What action must I take in response? _____
_____
_____

What am I learning about myself? _____
_____
_____

What did I do this week that I am proud of? _____
_____
_____

WHEN I GROW UP I WANT TO BE SIGNIFICANT

REMEMBER WHEN YOU WERE A KID AND THE TEACHER ASKED YOU what you wanted to be when you grew up? What did you say?

I wanted to be a jet pilot or a chiropractor. Alas, when I took those dang aptitude tests I had nothing going for me in either of those occupations, so my counselor suggested something in the helping professions. Thank goodness for strengths tests!

As I look back, I now see that I dreamed about being a jet pilot or a chiropractor because of the significance I attached to people in those fields. My dad loved planes, so that was a great way to bond with him as we met interesting pilots from all over the world. My chiropractor cared for me during my parents' divorce.

> "When someone is pursuing their dream, They'll go far beyond what seems to be their limitations."
>
> — Robert J. Kriegel

My real desire, you see, was to make a similar difference in people's lives. Without counsel I could have easily slipped into a career area I would struggle to be satisfied in — and end up merely surviving every day. This would have left little energy and resources to contribute to the betterment of the people I so wanted to help in the first place.

Today, I have the most interesting job this side of a psych ward. I absolutely love what I do and that is because what I truly desired as a kid is coming true in a way that I was uniquely wired to do.

Are you doing what you love?

What do you love about leading people? Is it for your own glory, or do you enjoy seeing your life make a difference in someone else's life? For many, the reward of leadership is the power and opportunity to creatively solve complex problems and see profitable results.

Of course, there are immature leaders who are still in their ego-blinded state, believing that it's about money, status, and power. Those folks don't last very long. The leaders who last are the ones who have something greater than themselves in mind. Their significance comes from knowing their life has made a difference in someone else's life.

What difference will you make this week?

YOUR WEEKLY RESPONSE

What is my leadership intention this week? _____
_____
_____

How I will benefit from this shift? _____
_____
_____

What might hinder my success? _____
_____
_____

What action must I take in response? _____
_____
_____

What am I learning about myself? _____
_____
_____

What did I do this week that I am proud of? _____
_____
_____

WAKE UP, EINSTEIN

"Sis, you'll keep gettin' whatch'r gettin' if you keep doin' whatch'r doin'."

That was my dad quoting Albert Einstein at me when I was an eight-year-old. I looked at him like, *What are you talking about!?* I soon got the point: I had better change my attitude or discipline was on the way!

Now that I'm an adult, lessons and discipline look different. But the same principle applies: Actions breed consequences. And attitude breeds actions.

Are you struggling with your "doin' and gettin' "? The fact is, disappointment, frustration, and stress will continue if you don't do something different. What behavior are you clinging to that is not working?

"I like a person who knows his own mind and sticks to it; who sees at once what, in given circumstances, is to be done, and does it."
— William Hazlitt

Perhaps it's control. (To be politically correct, we'll call it delegating.)

The problem with control is it camouflages itself behind a good image. Think of a super busy CEO, an über-organized mom, a rapid-growth entrepreneur. Each is getting a need met by staying in control while not letting go (i.e., by not asking for help which conveys vulnerability).

However, with so much pressure on them, they don't realize they've snapped emotionally, or are becoming resentful (either passively or aggressively). So they keep over-working, over-serving, over-dictating — which leads to exhaustion, and living from a triggered state of survival. And that results in addictions, isolation, bitterness, and burnout — which leads to the reinforced need to control. Can you see the insanity cycle?

How about you? Do you find you have high turnover in your organization, or a poorly motivated team, and wonder what's wrong with these people? Maybe you keep thinking, if you hire a new manager, things will be better. If you marry a new spouse, life will be better. If you had more money. If you get a new job. If you move...

I have liberating news for you. Wherever you go...there you are.

The common denominator to all your problems is *you*. And the secret to your success and happiness is not "out there" — it's *you*.

Nothing around you needs to change to make you happy and fulfilled. You need the power and desire to make new choices. You can do something different and get different results, but you must want to change your attitude, "your story," and your belief systems — for that is what drives your behavior, Einstein!

What could be different today if you made one small change?

YOUR WEEKLY RESPONSE

What is my leadership intention this week? _____
_____
_____

How I will benefit from this shift? _____
_____
_____

What might hinder my success? _____
_____
_____

What action must I take in response? _____
_____
_____

What am I learning about myself? _____
_____
_____

What did I do this week that I am proud of? _____
_____
_____

COMMUNICATION THEORY 101

IT HAS BEEN SAID THAT WORDS HOLD THE POWER OF LIFE AND DEATH. The more I coach leaders, the more convinced I am that this is true — culturally, mentally, emotionally.

Take a look at your leadership style. Many leaders do not know how to use their words to build others up, address conflict proactively and communicate what is in their heart. The result? Any thoughts of gratitude and appreciation get locked up in your head and never leave your mouth. Are you like this?

"Words can destroy. What we call each other ultimately becomes what we think of each other, and it matters."

— Jeane J. Kirkpatrick

What blocks the communication? You may be a wonderful communicator at the podium, with PowerPoint, on conference calls, or in front of your board of directors. Yet those closest to you don't feel valued. Instead of showing your sincere appreciation, you hide in your next safe task. Why aren't you more effective with your individual staff and team members? (And spouse and children?)

I'm not trying to be your shrink, but I do want to suggest that communication failure has to do with your unwillingness to be (or the unawareness of the need to be) honest with *yourself.* To be affirming and encouraging of others requires vulnerability on your part. Leaders' self-talk is often harsh and downright mean — that has to stop if you want to lead others well.

Let's be realistic. For some people, words come readily and flow off their tongue. For others it is unnatural and awkward and hard. The problem is not lack of skill. (That is forgivable.) It is lack of willingness to venture into a place of potential exposure and weakness. Leaders of organizations are given training on financial reports, and experience teaches them their unique tactical advantage. But the art of influence and caring for people — that is not something you can learn in isolation by reading a book or Googling leadership. You learn it by self-discovery, courage and authenticity.

Speak your words, write your words, use your words to communicate your care, your value, and your delight in those around you.

Right now, think of the people in your life who need your words of encouragement and write down the first two names that come to mind. Now act on that and communicate to them how much you appreciate and respect them. It will only take a minute!

The ROI is priceless.

YOUR WEEKLY RESPONSE

What is my leadership intention this week? _____
_____
_____

How I will benefit from this shift? _____
_____
_____

What might hinder my success? _____
_____
_____

What action must I take in response? _____
_____
_____

What am I learning about myself? _____
_____
_____

What did I do this week that I am proud of? _____
_____
_____

AVOIDING THE BUMP IN THE ROAD

ONE DAY I WAS DRIVING DOWN SNOQUALMIE PASS WHEN I RAN OVER something on Interstate 90. Nothing happened at first, so I thought I was okay, and smugly began to praise my SUV. Then I heard the faint sound of thumping.

I took my hands off the wheel to see if the Jeep was swerving, or if I had a chance to make it to the exit one mile down the road. The thumping got louder and I smelled smoke, so I made myself pull off to take a look. I called my stepdad who is a mechanic and tried not to cry. With him on my cell phone, we did a little troubleshooting. The front tires looked okay. Was it the brakes? Was something lodged in the undercarriage?

"Try not to become a man of success but rather try to become a man of value."

— *Albert Einstein*

Then I saw the back right tire. It was totally destroyed. I felt so dumb. I called a tow truck.

In an hour or so I was eating popcorn in the Les Schwab Tires waiting room, contemplating things. Like, why hadn't I pulled over at the first thump? The question has stayed with me. Maybe you can relate.

At the first sign of trouble, why don't we don't just pull over to evaluate? Nope, we entrepreneurs put on the gas! "If only I can make it to..." whatever the next goal is, we think, "then I'll pull over and deal with" this problem, team issue, personal conflict, habit, addiction, whatever you need to deal with.

Then, if avoiding the problem doesn't work, we finally stop. However, in our zest to go straight to where we believe the problem is, we fixate on the wrong thing. By then, time and resources are poured into solutions that are not solving the right problem, and we're still stuck on the side of the freakin' road!

I want to suggest that this doesn't have to happen. When people, like companies, live by their values and honor their purpose, decisions are made fast and accurately, avoiding expensive mistakes, costly time-stealers and wasted resources.

So I need to say it. Get clear on your values so you can have clarity to deal with all the problems, opportunities, and challenges that are headed your way.

Then, when you hit a bump, hear a thump, or smell smoke, pull over, for goodness sake!

What is one issue you can address this week?

YOUR WEEKLY RESPONSE

What is my leadership intention this week? _____
_____
_____

How I will benefit from this shift? _____
_____
_____

What might hinder my success? _____
_____
_____

What action must I take in response? _____
_____
_____

What am I learning about myself? _____
_____
_____

What did I do this week that I am proud of? _____
_____
_____

HASTE MAKES WASTE

WHAT IS SLOWLY LEAKING UNDER THE SURFACE OF YOUR LIFE?

I was camping at a lake with my friend, TG. He had been working on his boat for months and wanted to get it on the water before the weekend, to avoid the crowds (and to avoid the embarrassment of a large audience, should anything go wrong!).

On Tuesday, he did a trial run and found some leakage. Back to dry dock it went. TG's mechanic told him that he needed two pipes welded. TG got a second opinion from another guy who said, "Nah, just put a silicon seal around 'er and she'll hold." The quick fix won out and the boat was launched on Friday morning.

"An optimist is one who makes the best of it when he gets the worst of it."

— Laurence Peter

Saturday morning, TG got a call, and when we saw the look on his face we knew something horrible had happened. We piled into our trucks and tore up to the lake. When we got there, all we could see of the boat was the American flag fluttering just above the water line.

It is a long story of how we got that sucker out of the water, but let me just say that the same crowd that TG had wanted to avoid were now taking pictures and making jokes as they downed their Coronas.

Have you ever ignored warning signs? In my work with entrepreneurs, I ask them what their gut tells them, and then what their spouse or family has advised. Often they are so overwhelmed with self-imposed expectations, and ego to achieve and unrealistic deadlines, they are not listening to either. What usually follows is first exhaustion from working an obsession, then haste to get the deal over with, and then, a result parallel to TG's: sunk, embarrassed, and out of commission.

You may laugh at TG's story, but remember there was no sign of leakage when he was observing the boat. It sunk when he wasn't looking, convinced all was well. By the time someone noticed, it was too late.

Slow down and listen to that small voice inside telling you where the leaks in your life are so that you do not damage the very things that bring the greatest joy.

YOUR WEEKLY RESPONSE

What is my leadership intention this week? _____
_____
_____

How I will benefit from this shift? _____
_____
_____

What might hinder my success? _____
_____
_____

What action must I take in response? _____
_____
_____

What am I learning about myself? _____
_____
_____

What did I do this week that I am proud of? _____
_____
_____

REACHING THE TOP TOGETHER

Do you like to hike? I love it! One time my aunt and uncle came to town to conquer a few of the local hikes. Of course, we chose a super tough hike to tackle. In fact, the website said (and I quote) "The last mile is the mile from Hell!"

I admit I was a late adopter of the whole hiking sticks thing. Before "sticks," I had always been able to climb to the top on my own, right? Why carry something extra? Then I got some for my birthday. At first I only used them for descending, to ease my knees. Then came that "mile from hell" hike. Those sticks were not only a knee-saver, I couldn't have crossed the rivers or reached the top without them!

"The most important single ingredient in the formula of success is knowing how to get along with people."

— Theodore Roosevelt

Here's what I realized: I had never climbed a hard enough mountain to fully appreciate their value.

My shift in thinking reminded me of my clients who struggle with understanding the value of investing in people. Are you task-oriented or people-oriented?

Leaders who are focused on conquest and the next goal may think that taking the time to invest in people will add to the weight they are carrying, slow them down, or simply is not necessary to get where they want to go.

The wake-up call occurs when they want to go higher only to realize they are in that "last mile from hell" without any support.

Get to the next level by learning the art of investing in people. Determine their strengths and put them in positions where they can do their best. You may be able to get to the top either way, but at what cost?

Use your team of valued and efficient people to help carry the weight and help them get on their way to the next, higher, mountain!

And remember, it is not just about the conquest, but also the journey. Those sticks allowed me to be balanced as I crossed the rivers and gave me something to rest my weight on as I stair-climbed up the mountain on loose terrain. I could keep my head up and enjoy the beautiful view.

It is much more rewarding to get to the top of the mountain and share your experience with others than to show up by yourself, exhausted!

YOUR WEEKLY RESPONSE

What is my leadership intention this week? _____
_____
_____

How I will benefit from this shift? _____
_____
_____

What might hinder my success? _____
_____
_____

What action must I take in response? _____
_____
_____

What am I learning about myself? _____
_____
_____

What did I do this week that I am proud of? _____
_____
_____

THE MESSAGE OF ANGER

HERE'S A LITTLE QUIZ FOR YOU. WHICH IS MORE HARMFUL? PASSIVE or aggressive anger? Verbal or silent frustration? Hurt feelings voiced or stuffed?

The answer? All of the above. You've heard the cliché: Anger is one letter short of danger. All of those feelings and actions can be dangerous.

Is there a "good" anger? A rightful place for anger? Yes! Think of fire. When fire is intentional and controlled, it can be wonderful, even life-giving. If not, it's destructive and deadly.

> "Do not teach your children never to be angry; teach them how to be angry."
>
> — Lyman Abbott

Many of us have a natural short fuse. We get mad fast and get over it fast. Others have a long fuse. However, when they do get mad, it has been brewing inside for so long that when they blow, it is ugly! Then they take a long time to get over it.

The short and long of it is, we all need help with anger management. But we also need to go one step further and ask, *Is there something else our anger may be telling us?*

Anger is merely an emotion or reaction that something you want or desire is not happening. Psychologist Dr. Dan Allender explains that "Anger is our response to an assault. Its intensity is usually in accord with the degree of perceived injustice, though the assault need not be real or severe to draw forth an extreme response."*

Now when I get mad, I use the injustice formula to help me walk through my emotion. What do I perceive the injustice to be here? To be honest, most of the time the "injustice" is that my expectation was not met, or my desires were thwarted.

What makes you angry? What gets you fired up? You see, our purpose is wrapped up in helping others. Often the injustices that bring us the greatest spike of emotion are the very thing we were meant to go solve.

Take a moment today to check on your experience with your anger, and discern what it means. Then what one thing could do today to remove one injustice from the world? One smile given, one compliment emailed, one burden lifted.

* Dan B. Allender and Tremper Longman III, *The Cry of the Soul: How Our Emotions Reveal Our Deepest Questions About God* (NavPress, 1999)

YOUR WEEKLY RESPONSE

What is my leadership intention this week? _____
_____
_____

How I will benefit from this shift? _____
_____
_____

What might hinder my success? _____
_____
_____

What action must I take in response? _____
_____
_____

What am I learning about myself? _____
_____
_____

What did I do this week that I am proud of? _____
_____
_____

A LIFE OF INTEGRITY

My mom never had a written list of goals, but she had a clear vision for her children's lives. She knew how she wanted us to turn out and the role she needed to play to get us there. One of those goals was to train us to be responsible adults.

I learned that one while cleaning the toilet.

Earlier that day, Mom had overheard a woman trash-talk a teenager she had hired to clean her office. The girl was clueless on how to clean. So my mom called me into the bathroom to ensure I knew how to scrub a toilet "the right way." As I complained, she silenced me by saying it was her job as my mother to train me so when I left the house no one would ever call me clueless behind my back.

> "Some people procrastinate so much that all they can do is run around like firefighters all day-putting out fires that should not have gotten started in the first place."
> — Nido Qubein

You can bet I know how to clean toilets thoroughly and a few other life skills my mother drilled into me. Most of all, I learned to live a life of integrity by watching Mom.

You want to live a life of integrity, or you wouldn't be bothering to read this book. What do you want to be known for today and remembered for in the future? Is today the day to take a moment to be intentional? Could you invest one hour a week this year to get clear about who you are and what your vision is? How about the vision for the next generation?

Here's a place to start: What is your personal mission statement? Can you say it in seven words or less? Just as companies need a mission statement, we personally do as well. For what unique purpose are you here on earth, at this time in history, with your unique personality, talent and gifts in the roles are you playing?

Next, what about your family? Do your kids know your family's mission statement and why you as a family exist? Do you wake up in the morning and know what your primary roles require of you and how you intend to make a difference in the lives of others?

Remember, integrity is when your words, thoughts, and actions are in alignment. So, back to excuses and your to-do lists. What are you cluttering your day with? Are your thoughts and actions in alignment? Get back to your mission, your purpose, and focus on the important stuff. Today.

YOUR WEEKLY RESPONSE

What is my leadership intention this week? _____
_____
_____

How I will benefit from this shift? _____
_____
_____

What might hinder my success? _____
_____
_____

What action must I take in response? _____
_____
_____

What am I learning about myself? _____
_____
_____

What did I do this week that I am proud of? _____
_____
_____

WEEK 20: CHARACTER

THE MEEK AND WILD

WHAT'S YOUR INITIAL REACTION TO THE WORD *MEEK*?

I love the old movie, *The Man from Snowy River*. In it the main character, Jim Craig, not only tames a powerful, dangerous and beautiful wild colt, he captures the whole mob of brumbies, the term for feral horses in Australia. How? Only with the help of his faithful saddle horse, the real hero of the story.

Because its strength and power had been bridled, trained, and controlled, Craig's horse could carry him where other cowboys had not dared to go. It had the potential to go wild, to return to the herd, but it was obedient and loyal to Craig, part of a two-creature team on an outrageous mission. Was the meek saddle horse any less of a brave leader than the scene-stealing, bucking black brumbie?

> "What a man thinks of himself, that is what determines, or rather indicates, his fate."
> — Henry David Thoreau

Meekness is not spinelessness or sentimentality. The term *meek* comes from the Greek word *praus*, which is used for a strong beast that has been tamed. In other words, strength under control. Translated, you, in control.

Many times, we as leaders think we have to do the rearing-head colt-thing to get things done, yet isn't it the humble power of a mentor we remember? Test it, list the qualities of someone who has influenced your life in a meaningful way. If you are like most, your list will include integrity, humble confidence, gentle strength, and genuine interest in the good of others — a team player who invested in you.

Perhaps you've come to realize that rearing your head with loud "neighing" does little to control and motivate your team for long-term

40

purposeful change? Would you agree that controlled strength, tamed gentleness, and honest humility are valuable keys to powerful leadership? Want a little coaching tip...you can't fake it. A mask of careful words and calm demeanor won't last when the real heat comes on.

As long as the wild horse is standing still, he's not dangerous. But provoked, his true nature will be unleashed. Wild colts are independent and "edgy," but the reality is they are feared and dreaded, leaving destruction in their path.

That's not the legacy you want to leave, is it? Humility by having your strength under control or disciplined is the goal. Consider meekness as a character trait to develop and then you will leave a legacy as a leader who influenced and touched lives.

Remember, blessed are the meek.

YOUR WEEKLY RESPONSE

What is my leadership intention this week? _____
_____
_____

How I will benefit from this shift? _____
_____
_____

What might hinder my success? _____
_____
_____

What action must I take in response? _____
_____
_____

What am I learning about myself? _____
_____
_____

What did I do this week that I am proud of? _____
_____
_____

JUMPING OFF THE HAMSTER WHEEL

I HATE TO WASTE TIME. I HATE IT WHEN PEOPLE WASTE MY TIME. I really hate it when I waste someone else's time. I did that the other day, and it taught me something.

I had forgotten that I had scheduled a walk with a friend. Her response was gracious, though: "It's okay, I've actually got a ton of stuff done, so I considered it a gift of stress relief of a different sort."

Then it hit me, and maybe you'll relate to this too: I secretly love it when an appointment gets cancelled. Why? Because it gives me a window of time to accomplish some important, non-urgent but nagging tasks.

Now, if you're super-disciplined, don't point smugly to your quadrants and Outlook calendar blocking tools. I know that stuff, and, in fact, teach it often to folks just like you <grin>.

> "Nothing is so fatiguing as the hanging on of an uncompleted task."
> — William James

What I'm talking about is this. There is something in the entrepreneurial brain that requires this "free" zone, this space to be super creative, and routine is the enemy of it. Time plays either foe or friend to the creativity necessary to solve problems and ignite passion. Sometimes the weight of the deadline forces creativity to burst forth in squeezed-out brilliance. Other times, we are so tired from running on fumes and carrying the weight of the world on our shoulders there is no creativity to be found anywhere, especially when we need it.

If you have burned yourself out from too much on the plate, you are paying the personal price for not using your time wisely. Maybe you can identify with the downward spiral from running on adrenaline to high-functioning depression to pounding out more work to crashing on the weekend back to adrenaline on Monday. Once we're spinning on that spiral, we lose the creative ability to get out of the cycle. So we just keep running with the promise "as soon as… then I'll…." it will be back to normal.

Unfortunately, hamster-wheel living becomes "normal" and we silently give into just "keeping up."

The answer is simple. Stop!

Stop the madness and make the moments. Better yet, let the moments find you. In the cancelled appointment, the hum of the airliner, or the white noise of the coffee shop. Right now, look at your week and carve out at least three moments of creative white space. Then watch what happens!

YOUR WEEKLY RESPONSE

What is my leadership intention this week? _____
_____
_____

How I will benefit from this shift? _____
_____
_____

What might hinder my success? _____
_____
_____

What action must I take in response? _____
_____
_____

What am I learning about myself? _____
_____
_____

What did I do this week that I am proud of? _____
_____
_____

MISCOMMUNICATION AND OTHER RELATIONAL HAZARDS

A FRIEND AND I WERE VACATIONING IN MEXICO WHEN THE TOUR guide began rattling off instructions in Spanish faster than a Gatling gun. I know enough Spanish to get me to *los banos* but that's about it. So I turned to my friend and asked, "What did he say?" I was stunned when he answered by repeating what the guide indeed said — in Spanish.

For a moment I just stared at him, silently judging him to be an idiot. Then I said, "I mean, what did he say, *in English*, por favor?"

"The most important thing in communication is to hear what isn't being said."

— Peter Drucker

Something definitely went wrong in getting my request met. Was it my fault? No. But here is the catch — was it my friend's fault? No. He did exactly what I asked him to do. Was I disappointed for that split second? Yes. Did he think he had delivered what I needed? Yes. Was it what I wanted? No.

My friend and I got our wires uncrossed, laughed about it, and moved on. Sometimes it's not that easy.

Communication requires relationships, and vice versa. Every day I witness pain in business interaction, and a majority of it is relationship based. Thus, I want you to be passionate about effective communication, because trust is the key to growing healthy relationships.

Trust-building communication starts with knowing yourself, your behavioral style, and your communication filters and blocks. We need to recognize that we're surrounded by people who are not like us. (Duh!) In fact, approximately 75 percent of the population does not process information and situations like you do.

For instance, it is easy to see how miscommunication can happen if you are task-oriented and another person is people-oriented. What happens if you talk in bullet points starting with the bottom-line, and your listener wants to take in the full picture, hear all the details, and arrive at the conclusion through an analytical process. How different is that?

Slow down and watch for the nonverbal clues. If you think an exchange went wrong or even suspect it did, stop and ask questions. Try this: In a humble, teachable voice, ask, "What did you just hear me say?" Listen carefully, then own it (do not defend yourself) and restate what you meant to communicate.

Lastly, when you don't get what you need from an important conversation, you may need to laugh and say, "In English, please!"

YOUR WEEKLY RESPONSE

What is my leadership intention this week? _____
_____
_____

How I will benefit from this shift? _____
_____
_____

What might hinder my success? _____
_____
_____

What action must I take in response? _____
_____
_____

What am I learning about myself? _____
_____
_____

What did I do this week that I am proud of? _____
_____
_____

HOW DO YOU SPELL RELIEF?

RELIEF IS ONE OF MY FAVORITE EMOTIONS. YOU KNOW THE FEELING when you are 10 minutes late and finally find your keys?

Or here's one: I love it when I need to quickly communicate something too long to text but don't have time to talk, and I get the person's voicemail and can just leave a message. Ahh! Or more dramatically, consider the great wave of feeling when you can't find your child in the store and then finally catch sight of two little legs sticking out from under a clothes rack. Whew!

"Life isn't about waiting for the storm to pass, it's about learning how to dance in the rain."

— Gary Lee Walker

Relief definitely has its place. But it should never substitute for needed change.

How do you handle the need for change? Are you making changes — for simple relief or for real gain? Are you taking action that will lead to sustainable growth, or are you blowing smoke just to gain a reprieve, and then go back to business as usual when the crisis is over? People know the difference (they probably call it your "flavor of the month").

Relief for relief sake (vs. relief until real change can happen) will "off ramp" your success in the long run. Keep relief as the reward of true change instead of an ends unto itself.

Let's face it, when we experience an unexpected setback — or, for goodness sake, the uncertainty in the economy is reason enough — we need to trim all the fat we can and hunker down to the bare minimum. But what I want is to challenge you to examine your leadership style *today*, not against the backdrop of your personal drama and media headlines but your own heart of hearts. I want you to set yourself up for real growth and to help you stop reacting like a pinball machine to the latest financial forecasts.

These are the times that test and reveal your character as it is today. How you respond forges your character for tomorrow. You will either fly with eagles, or float with jelly fish. If there was ever a time to know yourself and work on your emotional intelligence and people skills, it is now.

So do not let another week go by! What needs to change? What nagging hindrance needs to be dealt with to bring you the right kind of relief!

YOUR WEEKLY RESPONSE

What is my leadership intention this week? _____

_____

_____

How I will benefit from this shift? _____

_____

_____

What might hinder my success? _____

_____

_____

What action must I take in response? _____

_____

_____

What am I learning about myself? _____

_____

_____

What did I do this week that I am proud of? _____

_____

_____

REAL RISK IN RELATIONSHIP

GROWING UP IN THE SIERRA NEVADA MOUNTAINS, I HAD A FEW TOO many opportunities for adventure: jumping snowmobiles in the full moon, passing three logging trucks on a two-lane highway in a '71 Vega, leaping off 40-foot cliffs into the Feather River, and countless other "near death experiences." Let's just say that some adventures were cause for a visit to the chiropractor on Monday morning.

These days, I've traded adventure stunts for business tactics. Perhaps you're like me. A different type of risk defines us...until someone challenges us to look deeper, or within. We may be successful but are we wealthy in relationships?

"Life is either a daring adventure or it is nothing."

— Helen Keller

Intimacy is necessary for rich relationships. The only way to have true intimacy is to risk your "self" emotionally. At this point, the risk-taker in many of us comes to a screeching halt. Thinking of exposing our inner being is enough to send half of us running!

Have you felt a gap within you? You want love, but as you pull people in, your attempt for true intimacy is sabotaged. The fear of rejection and the risk of truly being yourself unconsciously pushes love away, creating a gap.

Here's the sad part. We medicate the gap. With work, alcohol, food, pornography, shopping, bad relationships, adrenaline sports, travel and vacations, and even the latest pharmaceutical drug marketed to us. We keep our brain just busy enough that we don't have to connect to our heart. Our public persona is beautifully rewarded, so we keep medicating the gap. Yet our "true" self is never quite fulfilled and is left searching for significance and purpose.

So how do you bridge the gap toward real intimacy? Decide to build up enough emotional strength to be authentic and trust another. Maybe you start by trusting your closest friend, or maybe you start by trusting God. You must start somewhere and yes, you might get hurt. But denying truth doesn't change its reality. Risk may bring pain, but risk also brings freedom and reward.

I want you to have the freedom to love and to be loved. When you are ready to take a risk emotionally, then you are ready to open up your heart and soul. Develop a team of safe people to support you in your new venture.

Decide to be a true risk taker, today.

YOUR WEEKLY RESPONSE

What is my leadership intention this week? _____
_____
_____

How I will benefit from this shift? _____
_____
_____

What might hinder my success? _____
_____
_____

What action must I take in response? _____
_____
_____

What am I learning about myself? _____
_____
_____

What did I do this week that I am proud of? _____
_____
_____

EXPOSING OUR FOUNDATIONS

ON A TRIP TO THE COAST, I WAS WATCHING HOW THE EBB OF THE tide revealed sand and rocks previously concealed by the Pacific. It occurred to me that difficult times in our lives similarly expose our foundations, our true selves.

At low tide, everyone can see the ocean's once-hidden debris strewn across the beach. When the tide is high, the beautiful, shining water conceals the ugliness. The same is true in our lives. When things are good, we are not forced to look at what is going on inside our busy lives. But when the crisis hits and the tide recedes, not only do we have to face ourselves, but the whole world seems to take a peek too. We're left battered and uncertain, perhaps even depressed.

"Great crisis produce great men and great deeds of courage."
— John F. Kennedy

Maybe you've heard the wise maxim: *When disappointment hits we have a choice to become bitter or better. The only difference is the I.*

What's going on in your life that provides you an opportunity for some great character formation? How you respond to circumstances is your choice. Whether you are running a $250 million company or sweeping floors at the neighborhood church building — all of us need to improve our character. Are you up for some growth? Or are you resisting your situation? When life is not progressing as we'd hoped, or people are not living up to our expectations, we can choose to allow the hardness in our heart to be softened.

Consider your admired heroes, strong leaders, and personal role models. As you examine the character of these people, you will find a quiet humility formed from hard times — a brokenness, if you will. I'm willing to bet that when their weaknesses were revealed, they did not cover them up; they grabbed the opportunity to grow.

That's why effective leaders have the ability to serve and appreciate others while at the same time enabling them to achieve greatness. Do you want to be a more effective leader? Do you want to inspire greatness?

Yes, our world is continually being pounded by crises, wars, and downturns. But you can make a decision to hope and grow. Go get your feet wet.

YOUR WEEKLY RESPONSE

What is my leadership intention this week? _____
_____
_____

How I will benefit from this shift? _____
_____
_____

What might hinder my success? _____
_____
_____

What action must I take in response? _____
_____
_____

What am I learning about myself? _____
_____
_____

What did I do this week that I am proud of? _____
_____
_____

DON'T KILL YOUR CURIOSITY

WHEN MY NIECE KYLIE WAS TWO YEARS OLD, I HELPED HER DISCOVER her shadow.

As she interacted with it for the first time in her life, this auntie watched with pure joy. Ah, to be young again.

There's a part of being young, though, that we can, and should, still be practicing: Curiosity.

Curiosity is an emotion, and driven by that emotion, you are led to explore, investigate, and learn. That explains why people who shut off their emotions and live from their head, turn off their natural curiosity and settle for fact-finding. It also explains why one of the most powerful traits of a successful leader is a healthy curiosity.

"Twenty years from now you will be more disappointed by the things that you didn't do than by the ones you did do... Sail away from the safe harbor. Catch the trade winds in your sails. Explore. Dream. Discover."

— Mark Twain

Like children, great people have an inherent desire to learn from their environment. This hunger drives them to ask questions and explore how all this new information affects their organization.

Problems can arise when childlike curiosity gets confused with childlike behavior and leaves behind discipline and accountability. Think about it. Children are free to indulge their curiosity because they have a loving authority figure setting boundaries and averting any steps toward danger.

Unwise leaders think they must know the answers and go it alone. There is no parent around to yank you from the situation your curiosity led you into. Leaders fall the hardest because they have not placed themselves in relationships where they receive honest feedback on their behavior.

Where are you on the curiosity chart? When was the last time you just laid on the grass and let yourself ponder the clouds, the birds, or the wind? Or, has your curiosity led you down a road where you are no longer experiencing joy? Then get into a coaching or mentoring relationships today that will keep you from killing your curiosity but instead controlling it to produce greatness in your life.

Are you at a healthy place in your curiosity? Then celebrate and acknowledge to yourself this great trait in yourself and allow it to lead you to do something great for someone else. There is so much more to learn, so be curious and then courageous!

YOUR WEEKLY RESPONSE

What is my leadership intention this week? _____
_____
_____

How I will benefit from this shift? _____
_____
_____

What might hinder my success? _____
_____
_____

What action must I take in response? _____
_____
_____

What am I learning about myself? _____
_____
_____

What did I do this week that I am proud of? _____
_____
_____

CAN YOU WIN AT DEFENSE?

ON THE BASKETBALL COURT I LOVE PLAYING DEFENSE. I CAN BE pretty good at it too. I need to be, because I can't shoot. The only way I add value to the team is to play a hard defense and pass aggressively to my teammates. That makes me look like a great team player, but it doesn't help the team win over the long haul. I need to be able to drive it in and score.

My defensive façade hides the fact that I am too lazy to practice my shot and not motivated enough to get a coach to help me.

And do you know what? I find myself doing the same thing in life and business: excelling at defense to cover up laziness and lack of skill.

Are you playing zone defense, or the full court?

Since a portion of my work involves conflict resolution, I witness defensiveness every day of the week. Both leaders and followers use defensive techniques in their game around the table: intimidation, aggressive silence, false guilt, and non-verbal daggers, for instance.

"Of all the liars in the world, sometimes the worst are your fears."

— Rudyard Kipling

Being the queen bee of defensiveness myself, it is not hard to discern what buttons are being pushed. Fear of being taken advantage of, fear of loss of security, fear of unwarranted criticisms, fear of being found out, fear of making a mistake, and — my personal favorite — fear of rejection. The list goes on.

Does any of this strike close to home?

We forget that we should be defending against opponents — not our own teammates. From a place of fear we set up a screen to protect ourselves. In both passive and aggressive ways we hide and isolate ourselves from truth that could bring healing and restoration to a huge pain in the team. The more talented we are at our defensive maneuvers, the more we fool ourselves that we are good team players — that is until we get passed the ball and it is up to us to score.

May you be encouraged to let your guard down with your team so you can play the game together, knowing it's not each other you are defending yourselves against.

Who on your team or in your family do you need to be more vulnerable and authentic with to get past the block that is hindering your personal success and fulfillment?

YOUR WEEKLY RESPONSE

What is my leadership intention this week? _____
_____
_____

How I will benefit from this shift? _____
_____
_____

What might hinder my success? _____
_____
_____

What action must I take in response? _____
_____
_____

What am I learning about myself? _____
_____
_____

What did I do this week that I am proud of? _____
_____
_____

BE WHO YOU ARE

FOR YEARS I TRIED TO BE A RUNNER. I WOULD STRIVE TO "PUSH through" the pain and get past "the wall." But I found myself getting prescriptions for physical therapy for my knees and ankles more than I was actually running.

Finally, a Pilates expert explained that my body's structure does not support running. I probably could be a pretty good swimmer, however. I knew she was right. I have always been a strong swimmer and love it (even though it's extremely inconvenient). Still, I left her office sad because I badly wanted to be a runner like my friends. It's so easy, convenient, and outdoors.

"Freedom to be your best means nothing unless you're willing to do your best."

— *Colin Powell*

The truth is, though, the first time I jumped back in the pool, I swam a half-mile and was ready for more. I learned a good lesson that day about life. I was able to give up the decade of struggle to find what my body was designed to do and could excel at something without suffering.

It made me look at all the other areas of my life I was trying to be something I am not.

You were designed to win a unique race in life. Call it your purpose, your destiny, your reason for being here. Your specific strengths, talents, gifts, behavior styles, motivators, physical being are all perfectly fitted for you to win *your* unique race.

My passion for coaching is fueled by my desire to see people live up to their full potential by discovering the race they were meant to win. I also want to help them train and be fit to run their life race. Having a team — a coach, a spouse, a mentor, your friends — to help you is the most efficient way to get started in this discovery.

It is time for you to *be you.* To be your best, and to run the race you were called to compete in. If not now, then when?

YOUR WEEKLY RESPONSE

What is my leadership intention this week? _____
_____
_____

How I will benefit from this shift? _____
_____
_____

What might hinder my success? _____
_____
_____

What action must I take in response? _____
_____
_____

What am I learning about myself? _____
_____
_____

What did I do this week that I am proud of? _____
_____
_____

KEEPING BUSY TO AVOID RESPONSIBILITY

KEEPING BUSY TO AVOID RESPONSIBILITY.

The universal sins of procrastination and martyrdom, wrapped up in one! Haven't we all been totally guilty of being busy versus intentional?

The more busy we seem, whether professionally or personally, the less responsibility we take for the results we are not achieving. We have all known the victim of a busy life who ends up unwilling to take responsibility for their actions, blaming other people for not pitching in, living a poor quality of life, and consistently avoiding key accountabilities all because they are so busy.

"Man must cease attributing his problems to his environment, and learn again to exercise his will — his personal responsibility."

— Albert Einstein

Leaders are the worst, I'm telling ya. They would rather get their fingers into everyone's stuff, declare their direct reports incompetent, and take things back into their control, than fulfill their own responsibilities of leading!

Leadership is about setting the vision, trusting and supporting the team you have put in place, and getting out in front of the company. But how many of us are guilty of letting that weight of responsibility send us running back to hiding from our fears of failure — back to where we last succeeded.

Don't be fooled by busy people. They may well be avoiding something important in their lives and probably can't see it for what it is. People with a clear vision and mission do not shirk from responsibility but lead confidently forward. They are driven, dedicated, and focused but from a value-driven, purposeful mentality.

When will we stop and take care of ourselves, and thus our responsibilities? When will we stop saying yes to things that allow us to circumvent our responsibilities because we are fearful of failure or rejection? The answer: When we choose to live a life of significance instead of avoiding the true life we were meant to live. I have decided not to allow people to call me busy, because. I'm not I am living a full, intentional life that is my choice and I am proud of.

Think about it. Do you admire, respect, and want to follow a leader who is running around with their hair on fire all the time? How much better to be aligned with leaders who are confident in who they are, where they are at, and what path they are leading down! Which do you want to be known for? Busy or intentional?

YOUR WEEKLY RESPONSE

What is my leadership intention this week? _____
_____
_____

How I will benefit from this shift? _____
_____
_____

What might hinder my success? _____
_____
_____

What action must I take in response? _____
_____
_____

What am I learning about myself? _____
_____
_____

What did I do this week that I am proud of? _____
_____
_____

GROWING TRUST

WHAT IS THE ONE THING YOU WANT TO CONCENTRATE ON FOR THE next ten years? Your one word intention for the next decade?

Go somewhere quiet and get yourself very still. Then ask, *What is the one thing that would get me closer to fulfilling my purpose and living my vision? What is the one thing that would make the biggest difference?*

Ironically, when I asked myself the decade question, the answer was trust.

I say ironic because as you have undoubtedly picked up I believe in trust, preach trust, and build trust all day long. Yet I feel I need more of it in my own life, and my intention is to grow it for the next decade.

> "Leadership must be demonstrated, not announced."
>
> — Fran Tarkenton

Why? Leaders who have learned to trust themselves take great pains to live lives of integrity. They do not compromise their values, they have accountability to others, and they do not think higher of themselves than they should but instead they have a very clear vision of themselves. Jim Collins calls it "humility," and it is a must for a Level 5 leader.

Humble leaders trust more easily because they realize that the world does not rest solely on their shoulders. They get it that they are not in ultimate control. It sounds weird, but while they are fully responsible and take ownership, unless they are narcissistic they understand they are not the highest authority in life. Even the most powerful leader is under some kind of authority.

For example, when as a leader you submit yourself to the authority of the vision and purpose of the business, there is relief. When done correctly, you are able to trust the agreed-upon purpose and plan to drive the behaviors and motivations of the company. This in turn makes it much easier for people to trust you. They can trust that you will not knee-jerk change the plan when the pressure gets to you or blow a gasket when something inevitably does not meet your expectations. You will deliver upon the vision and values of the company and you trust that everyone else is working toward the same purpose.

People want to follow that leader! When leaders have learned to yield to authority, they are much more equipped to wield authority.

What is your one word intention for the next decade?

YOUR WEEKLY RESPONSE

What is my leadership intention this week? _____
_____
_____

How I will benefit from this shift? _____
_____
_____

What might hinder my success? _____
_____
_____

What action must I take in response? _____
_____
_____

What am I learning about myself? _____
_____
_____

What did I do this week that I am proud of? _____
_____
_____

BALANCED BODY BUILDING

IF YOU SAW A COMPETITIVE BODY BUILDER WHOSE RIGHT ARM WAS massive and whose left looked as skinny as a 10-year-old's, what would you think? Something's out of balance, right?

The image illustrates what it's like when hard-charging business people apply energy and initiative at work, and then lose motivation outside the office.

Many of my friends and clients miss the connection of why their business success does not translate into fulfilling relationships with spouses, friends or kids. The desire is there, but these strong people look at me helpless and say that they are too tired to lead and be creative when they get home from a long day at the office. Yet one of the key reasons they're working so hard is to provide and care for their family and loved ones. Out of balance, indeed!

Even if you're on the right track you'll get run over if you just sit there."

— Will Rogers

We crave good feedback and the power of positive reinforcement is strong. People tell you at work how awesome you are and you start believing your own press. Soon you are so proud of your right arm and all the attention that you get from it that you unconsciously only show your best side hoping that no one will notice your wimpy side — you know, the one you have neglected. But don't fool yourself. Your pride in your strong side can blind you to your weakness, but in time most people can spot the lack of balance.

So what shape are your emotional biceps in?

Doing so many curls with that right arm that you have no energy left to build strength on your left side doesn't make sense, does it? Making a stab at pumping iron once or twice a month is a waste of time too. Only initiating a regular, balanced and healthy routine in all areas of your life will result in that defined left arm (e.g., personal relationships) *as well as* the right (e.g., business success). Soon you are so proud of your strong, symmetrical biceps you'll be strutting around in sleeveless shirts.

Be encouraged! The good news is that you can begin to balance out and make that personal side an integrated success immediately. You can choose to apply the initiating skills that brought you success in the marketplace toward the same level of success in your home and community.

What are you willing to invest to create more balance? It matters!

YOUR WEEKLY RESPONSE

What is my leadership intention this week? _____
_____
_____

How I will benefit from this shift? _____
_____
_____

What might hinder my success? _____
_____
_____

What action must I take in response? _____
_____
_____

What am I learning about myself? _____
_____
_____

What did I do this week that I am proud of? _____
_____
_____

PREPARING FOR SUCCESS

ONE SUMMER, WE SEATTLE-ITES RECEIVED WHAT WE OFTEN LONG for. A bit more than we long for, actually.

After nine long months of gray, sunshine broke through our perennial clouds and shone bright and shone hot. People actually started smiling and we all soaked it up, until it turned into a record-breaking heat wave. Then the whole city fell apart. Overworked ACs broke down and businesses had to close. People got grumpy from lack of sleep. No one bought hot coffee (that's a big deal in Seattle, you know). The only folks still smiling were transplants from Florida who considered us wimps.

"Doing what we were meant to do creates fun, excitement and contentment in our lives, and invariably, in the lives of the people around us. When you're excited about something it's contagious."

— Mark Victor Hansen

We sighed relief when the clouds came back. Too much of a good thing — or lack of preparing for what we really want — spells trouble.

So answer this question: What are you longing for in your heart of hearts to accomplish? If that wish, desire, or goal came true, would you be ready to accept and assimilate it into your life? What do you need to prepare for, and how? Will you despise the very thing you long for once it is yours in abundance?

People often chase vague goals imposed on them by phantom parental expectations or their own driving inner voice. But they have no real idea what "success" would look like, but by golly they are busting their butts to get there.

Why not get really clear on what you want and start preparing yourself to receive it joyfully, instead of just striving for "it," like the proverbial carrot on the stick? To make sure you reach the pinnacle of success

— and like who you are when you get there — you need to know who you are, where your identity lies, what motivates you, why you want what you want, and what desired result are you hoping for when you really get what you want!

Ask yourself the hard questions! Defining is the first step to being. Then identifying the next step to *be* the person who is ready to accept and live what you really want.

What is it you really, really want? Why? Now ask yourself why five more times? Hmmm... What did you just learn about yourself?

YOUR WEEKLY RESPONSE

What is my leadership intention this week? _____
_____
_____

How I will benefit from this shift? _____
_____
_____

What might hinder my success? _____
_____
_____

What action must I take in response? _____
_____
_____

What am I learning about myself? _____
_____
_____

What did I do this week that I am proud of? _____
_____
_____

REDEFINING F.E.A.R.

ONE OF THE GREATEST CHALLENGES WE FACE IS...FEAR.

Fear has an interesting place in life, as both a curse and a blessing. It keeps us from reaching our highest potential, and it keeps us from doing really dumb things (such as my buddy, who has no fear, bridge-jumping and bursting his ear drum).

Fear has been described as False Evidence Appearing Real. In my coaching practice, I find one of the main reasons people do not reach their goals is some form of fear. I have simultaneously worked with one client who had a fear of success, and another one who had a fear of failure. Interestingly enough, the result of these polar fears were identical: the inability to move toward what they really desired to accomplish. They were stuck, because they allowed fear to block the next step.

"Huge waves that would frighten an ordinary swimmer produce a tremendous thrill for the surfer who has ridden them. Let's apply that to our own circumstances. The things we try to avoid and fight against — tribulation, suffering, and persecution — are the very things that produce abundant joy in us."

— Oswald Chambers

Are you struggling with fear? What might unblock you and empower you to take that next step? Ambrose Redmoon said, "Courage is not the absence of fear, but rather the judgment that something else is more important than fear."

Fear is not the problem as much as the value we assign to it. For example, take a child who is too fearful to learn to ride a bike. "What if I fall?" she asks her parent. As an adult, we know that this may indeed happen so we extend all the support we can to keep it from happening and then offer comfort when it does happen. However, the lifelong skill of riding a bike is worth a little skinned-up knee in the beginning, isn't it? Fear is not the problem as much as the value we assign to it.

A healthy fear can be defined as "reverence or awe": think of fear of gravity or fear of God. After suffering from Chronic Fatigue for two years, I have a healthy fear (a.k.a. respect) of my body's limitations. I dare not push myself beyond a certain point, because I know what the results might be. *Ugh!* Yet, if I dwell too long on it I become fearful I will get sick again and hold back.

Remember, we need to be in tune to what our fear is telling us — and then we need tell it what we are going to do in response.

Are you allowing fear to block your progress or open the door to new opportunity?

YOUR WEEKLY RESPONSE

What is my leadership intention this week? _____
_____
_____

How I will benefit from this shift? _____
_____
_____

What might hinder my success? _____
_____
_____

What action must I take in response? _____
_____
_____

What am I learning about myself? _____
_____
_____

What did I do this week that I am proud of? _____
_____
_____

THE SILENT KILLER

SILENCE ISN'T GOLDEN. IT IS DESTRUCTIVE.

You may not realize it, but the problems you are facing right now at work or at home likely can be traced to silence. Huh?

We may live in an era of email and smart phones and wireless networks. Yet in virtually every employee survey, communication tops the "needs-improvement" list.

Problems in communication can mean inaccurate information or insensitive comments. But a huge chunk of it fits in the negative category of *not* communicating information. The *lack* of communication.

I have a client whose vice president has gone silent. The man is taking days to reply to e-mail messages and voicemails, is forgetting to include subject-matter experts in strategic meetings, and is not making crucial decisions.

"Act the way you'd like to be and soon you'll be the way you act."
— George W. Crane

My client hesitates to directly ask the VP, who in the past has shot down such questions. So my client finds himself filling in the blanks. He's questioning his own worth. Am *I* the problem? Should I start looking for another VP? And he's not the only one affected. The whole team's efficiency has halted, deadlines are being missed, morale is plummeting, rumors are flying — all because we have a VP who is unresponsive and "too busy" to deal with the team.

People don't like "dead air." You've seen it in conversation: people inevitably fill a too-long silence with a comment or question. It's the same in work and personal relationships, only on a larger scale. *People can't help "filling in the blanks" caused by lack of communication and leadership.* They speculate as to why the silence in so deafening. And soon the damage is done.

The truth is, trying not to cause problems by not doing any harm is not being a good leader. It's abdication. Not saying anything in fear you'll of saying the wrong thing is not only good communication. It's cowardice. If you're not leading, you are following. There are no extra credit points for not doing anything wrong, especially if you haven't done anything at all.

So take note: *You need to use your words*! Communicate or pay the price. To the listener *silence communicates* a lack of care, concern, and value. To the one being silent, you can't hide, you must face your fear of doing something wrong — and do something right.

YOUR WEEKLY RESPONSE

What is my leadership intention this week? _____
_____
_____

How I will benefit from this shift? _____
_____
_____

What might hinder my success? _____
_____
_____

What action must I take in response? _____
_____
_____

What am I learning about myself? _____
_____
_____

What did I do this week that I am proud of? _____
_____
_____

WHAT IS YOUR PERSONAL OPERATING SYSTEM?

WHENEVER MY OLD COMPUTER WOULD FREEZE, WHICH WAS frequently, I'd just reboot. I would never take the time to determine what the cause was. All those quick fixes eventually rendered useless the entire computer. I now have a MAC, but that is a whole other topic.

You may not have thought of it this way, but we all approach life with our own personal operating systems — the framework of who we are, which in turn drives everything we do. I want to suggest that many of our frustrations in life can be traced back to our OS getting out of whack and us mindlessly hitting CTRL-ALT-DEL hoping for a quick fix.

"Insanity: doing the same thing over and over again and expecting different results."
— Albert Einstein

When life slips out of balance, we may end up compromising our values and not living with integrity. Integrity means that our thoughts, words, and actions are in alignment. When our value system is compromised, we either withdraw as we face what's wrong, or we just continue to reboot causing physical damage to the hardware (our bodies).

For example, let's say that you value honesty. A conflict arises over money and you can't get your spouse to see it your way. You're feeling a bit guilty, so you begin to justify yourself, then spend more hours at the office, and before long there's a freeze in the system. Instead of investigating why you (the OS) have developed difficulty with your partner (the program), you rationalize that there must be a "glitch" in *their* system.

We react much like our anti-virus software, with a choice to either delete or repair the program. Too often, we simply hit OK to remove the "glitch." Only after the damage is done do we recall the pop-up warning box us that said we were about to delete an integral part of our system.

The crash soon follows. To cope, we go into "safe mode," isolating ourselves from intimacy. Or worse, we quickly "add" the next beautiful person (program), convinced that he/she well be glitch-free! Of course, the computer continues to crash, because the operating system is inadequate.

Power down for a few moments and list the top five areas where your thoughts, words, actions, and beliefs are not in alignment.

You can't be turned in for the latest model and a new OS, like my MAC, but you can upgrade your values and restore your integrity! Do it today.

YOUR WEEKLY RESPONSE

What is my leadership intention this week? _____
_____
_____

How I will benefit from this shift? _____
_____
_____

What might hinder my success? _____
_____
_____

What action must I take in response? _____
_____
_____

What am I learning about myself? _____
_____
_____

What did I do this week that I am proud of? _____
_____
_____

NAVIGATING THROUGH STRESS

HAVE YOU EVER BEEN RIVER RAFTING THAT IS ACTUALLY A RIVER float — a slow one at that? On a visit to Phoenix, I found myself on a relaxing two-hour trip down the Salt River. What I thought was going to be a whitewater adventure ended up being a good lesson learned.

Amongst my companions was a brilliant engineer friend who saw my eyes light up whenever we moved faster than molasses. She rattled off some foreign-sounding formula, which when translated simply meant for the same amount of water to flow through a smaller space it must go faster. Where the river is wide, the water has the liberty to move at a slower velocity. Instantly the illustration popped for me.

> *"Our greatest danger in life is in permitting the urgent things to crowd out the important."*
> — *Charles E. Hummel*

Of course, balanced living includes seasons of whitewater rapids, but is your entire life like a trip down a Class VI river? When your to-do list is overloaded, life can move so rapidly that you only have time to dodge boulders, let alone think. You may spend days simply reacting to the symptoms of a problem, when what you need are creative solutions to the source of it. Conversely, when your mental space is wider, you can begin to think creatively and live intentionally.

I love helping people tap into their creativity by generating more space in their mind. You can do this by learning to identify and eliminate "hindrances" — unnecessary small or large things that take up mental and emotional space in your life.

On the river, I gained so much more than another adrenaline rush. As my body relaxed and my brain settled down, I stared into the water and effortlessly solved a dilemma I have been struggling with for months. Soon all these ideas started flowing. Moments later I had the most amazing idea for my next business venture. More importantly, I spent time with some friends and could simply enjoy their company.

The few rapids were fun, but as I reflect back, it was the floating that restored my soul and refreshed my brain. I left the river with solutions and all because I floated in the wide area of the river.

So here's the challenge. What can you do this week to widen your river, clear some RAM in the brain, and rediscover the creativity that lies within you?

YOUR WEEKLY RESPONSE

What is my leadership intention this week? _____
_____
_____

How I will benefit from this shift? _____
_____
_____

What might hinder my success? _____
_____
_____

What action must I take in response? _____
_____
_____

What am I learning about myself? _____
_____
_____

What did I do this week that I am proud of? _____
_____
_____

SADDLE UP ANYWAY

JOHN WAYNE HAD IT RIGHT WHEN HE SAID, "COURAGE IS BEING scared to death and saddling up anyway."

Do you think of yourself as courageous? To show courage you must be in tune with your core values, understand your own fears and desires, committed to your integrity, and tenacious in your ability to live it all in the face of opposition.

Courage is not something you do. It comes from who you are.

Courage is not fearlessness. Courage is actually about being quite clear on what you fear and pressing through it to the other side. It's not risk taking. It's not strategic decision-making. It's about following your heart, analyzing facts, and believing that your integrity is what matters in the end. Courage is about leading the vision when the rest of the world wants to watch CNN for hints on their next move. Courage is about daily choices.

> "Courage is what it takes to stand up and speak; courage is also what it takes to sit down and listen."
>
> — Winston Churchill

It is doing the right thing especially when it makes you vulnerable to disapproval or public misunderstanding. Courage is about admitting you're wrong, taking responsibility, and owning the fallout of your choices.

Courage is becoming a lost art in leadership.

Without self-awareness and a keen understanding of our fears and desires, we will likely give in to our narcissism and self-delusion. For example, a CEO who is clueless to his underlying fear of rejection may dominate and rule others from a place of arrogance and self-protection. Such an attitude likely creates a reality in which no one trusts or respects this leader; they instead simply give lip service to get what they want.

I see good leaders firsthand get so busy and stressed out, they forget what they fear. They don't realize every decision they are rapidly making is a reaction to guard them from that fear. Then, as if no one can see through them, they cover up their actions so they don't have to face their fear. Not only is it ridiculous; it is being cowardly. You are more than that!

What is one area you know you need to face head-on with courage?

Listen to your coach. You have what it takes. Face your fears, take courage and saddle up.

YOUR WEEKLY RESPONSE

What is my leadership intention this week? _____
_____
_____

How I will benefit from this shift? _____
_____
_____

What might hinder my success? _____
_____
_____

What action must I take in response? _____
_____
_____

What am I learning about myself? _____
_____
_____

What did I do this week that I am proud of? _____
_____
_____

GIVERS OR TAKERS

I HAVE A FRIEND WHO NEEDS A HEART TRANSPLANT. IT HAS GOTTEN me thinking about givers and takers, and leadership and influence.

My friend is a giver. I have always looked at his needing a new physical heart because allegorically, he gave so much from his old heart that he wore it out.

What about you? If there was a line in the middle of a continuum, on which side would you stand? The giver side, or the taker side?

In what ways do you give? Do you give the way you want to, or the way the recipient needs you to give? In other words, do you believe you are giving (helping, contributing), but in reality are you actually taking (getting affirmation, doing payback, or gaining control)?

> *"Almost all our sorrows can be traced to relationships with the wrong people, and our joys to relationships with the right people."*
>
> — John C. Maxwell

I once had a session with a couple. The wife was an introvert who liked to process her answers before speaking. Her quick-thinking husband would fill those two seconds of silence by telling her what to do and why. He honestly thought he was being helpful. Wow!

Interestingly, the people with reputations for control, manipulation, and arrogance often actually believe they are being helpful. Deep inside they may hide a desire to give of themselves. However, they give with their heads, not their hearts. (And as a result, they feel grossly misunderstood, which produces anger, leading to self-protection and isolation. I bet you know one of these people — or perhaps are one.)

We need to get outside of our own need to give, and be mindful of the true needs around us, and then give sacrificially from our heart to meet that need. If we are not careful, we can get a "high" off of "giving" quick solutions "to save others from themselves." The tragedy is that this creates a false sense of purpose — to be the go-to smart guy who thinks he or she have the best solutions — and keep people at an arm's length.

I invite you into a journey toward giving from the heart, from your true essence. And when you get there, you will discover you need others, you need something bigger than yourself.

It is there that you will allow someone else a true joy, a true moment of greatness for them as they are able to give to you. They'll experience a sense of love and purpose — a new heart — which will draw people to you, not push them away.

YOUR WEEKLY RESPONSE

What is my leadership intention this week? _____
_____
_____

How I will benefit from this shift? _____
_____
_____

What might hinder my success? _____
_____
_____

What action must I take in response? _____
_____
_____

What am I learning about myself? _____
_____
_____

What did I do this week that I am proud of? _____
_____
_____

GUARANTEED NOT TO FAIL

WHAT WOULD YOU DO IF YOU COULD NOT FAIL?

On a lazy Sunday, I asked a few of my friends that question and was stunned at the things that poured forth. One friend would start dancing again; another would pursue an old relationship; another would launch a new service component in her business.

I had to ask the logical next question. What one small step could they each take that week toward their dream or goal? The room went silent. Why? Fear. Fear of success, fear of failure, fear of love, fear of rejection, and fear of the unknown.

"If we let things terrify us, life will not be worth living."

— *Seneca*

Fear is not necessarily bad, of course. The problem is that we often mistaken debilitating fear, which keeps us from fulfilling our purpose, with healthy fear, which keeps us from making unwise choices.

Debilitating fear keeps us from our own greatness. Think of this kind of fear as "False Evidence Appearing Real." Our "gut" tells us to step into something new and to trust. But we begin to think about all the things that "could" happen (false evidence) and convince ourselves that they will happen (appear real). So we let the opportunity go by and live with a sense of "what if" and regret.

If you have a sense of fear, ask yourself if the choice at hand would get you closer to the person you want to be. If the answer is no, then fear is your friend and you should listen carefully to what it is telling you. But if the answer is yes, then you need to push through, conquer the fear and not let it stop you.

Whenever I'm a keynote speaker, I have a twinge of fear because the audience is unknown, but after the first few minutes the fear is gone and I'm glad I showed up and proceed with confidence in my message.

What would you do today if fear was not an issue? If you did not fear failure what one thing would you do? If you were guaranteed success what would you attempt?

Why not take one baby step toward your greatness in the next 24 hours? Oh all right, how about the next seven days?

YOUR WEEKLY RESPONSE

What is my leadership intention this week? _____
_____
_____

How I will benefit from this shift? _____
_____
_____

What might hinder my success? _____
_____
_____

What action must I take in response? _____
_____
_____

What am I learning about myself? _____
_____
_____

What did I do this week that I am proud of? _____
_____
_____

HIDING BEHIND BUSYNESS

ARE YOU A BUSY PERSON? IS IT A GOOD KIND OF BUSY? IS THERE SUCH a thing as "good busy?"

Why do so many leaders love busyness? Maybe because most leaders despise weakness in themselves so they stay busy to stay important. Weakness is the last thing they want others to spot. So, instead of stepping up and taking responsibility in an area they are unsure of, they skirt it and hide behind another competency they feel confident in.

You may already realize that a lot of successful entrepreneurs are very good at the *doing* part of business (sales, technical, projects), yet they are not skilled in leading the team to do it and managing the team to get results. The easiest way to assure that no one discovers this is to stay busy, because somewhere along the way being "busy" is an excuse for not taking action.

Praise is a powerful people-builder. Catch individuals doing something right.

— Brian Tracy

Likewise, successful leaders in the workplace might unconsciously place more significance in work because they are unsure that they can succeed at home. They keep "busy" at work and hide behind their professional competency, abdicating where they could make the biggest impact for generations to come.

Strong leaders are not the ones *who do everything right.* They are the ones to put a plan together, take risks, make mistakes, humbly admit their mistakes, take responsibility for failures, make necessary changes, do not fear correction, and win the trust of their followers and the team of which they were leading!

You need to confront the areas you are fearful of and move *toward* them, not away from them. How? Put relationships and results ahead of looking perfect. Commit to connecting with others, in contrast to protecting yourself. Admit to those following you, "I am not completely certain of the best course, but this is where I am headed." Then seek input. You are hiring people who are brighter than you in many areas, aren't you?

What will emerge? The possibilities are endless!

People around you are waiting for your words of encouragement, your words of wisdom, and your gift of being "present."

YOUR WEEKLY RESPONSE

What is my leadership intention this week? _____
_____
_____

How I will benefit from this shift? _____
_____
_____

What might hinder my success? _____
_____
_____

What action must I take in response? _____
_____
_____

What am I learning about myself? _____
_____
_____

What did I do this week that I am proud of? _____
_____
_____

TO ERR IS HUMAN,
TO FORGIVE IS GOOD BUSINESS

Forgiveness? In the business world?

Late for a meeting, a manager is flying down the hall in "task-mode" and demands a quick answer from the marketing admin. The admin interprets this as downright insulting. The manager, of course, has no idea his behavior has been interpreted as offensive; he is just trying to put out fires. For the admin, the judgment of jerk has been issued, the seed of resentment planted and the taking up of offense has begun.

Soon, every time the manager walks into the room, the admin feels the anger, but since no words have been spoken the manager misunderstands the cold shoulder and distances himself, leaving the relationship to further break down. What is needed to mend this situation is some serious conflict resolution culminating in forgiveness!

"To forgive is to set a prisoner free and discover that the prisoner was you."

— Lewis B. Smedes

The best definition of forgiveness I have for the workplace is, *Giving up my right to hurt you, even though you hurt me.*

More often than not, the other person is not aware he or she has offended you. In reconciling, the first step is learning the other person's true intention. Usually, hearing their intention, you can see where the miscommunication occurred and then you must forgive and let it go. In a sense, it is a canceling of a debt owed. Forgiveness is letting someone go free even though they did you wrong. In reality, forgiveness actually sets *you* free.

The result of forgiveness? Relief — and release. When you forgive, you release health back into your body; you release creativity; and you release energy to flow through you to others. Lack of forgiveness quickly leads to bitterness. Bitterness has been proven to lead to sickness and fatigue.

By the way, forgiveness is instant but trust is not. Building trust back into the relationship takes successful experiences over time. Forgiveness must be granted freely but trust must be earned.

Where does one start? With yourself.

So many of us carry guilt, which is anger toward our own selves for mistakes we've made, hurt we've caused, and decisions we've chosen. The more you beat yourself up, the less love and forgiveness you have to grant others. If you find you're unable to forgive yourself, then that's a spiritual issue you need to take to someone bigger than you. If you need to apologize to another person and own your mistake, then do it now. Forgive yourself, and let the anger go. Each day you hold onto to unforgiveness you rob yourself of joy, health, and energy. Stop!

Touchy/feely? I don't think so. I think forgiveness is a missing key to corporate success. We have a lot of work to do here in the workplace. So when will you take the first step? How about today?

YOUR WEEKLY RESPONSE

What is my leadership intention this week? _____
_____
_____

How I will benefit from this shift? _____
_____
_____

What might hinder my success? _____
_____
_____

What action must I take in response? _____
_____
_____

What am I learning about myself? _____
_____
_____

What did I do this week that I am proud of? _____
_____
_____

TRUST STARTS WITH YOU

DO YOU TRUST YOURSELF? DO YOU TRUST YOUR DIRECT REPORTS AND team members?

These are not rhetorical questions. Stephen M.R. Covey has boldly stated that the number one leadership competency in the new global economy is trust. It's that crucial.

Teams without trust can easily waste 10 to 40 hours a week in productivity. Seriously, what is that costing your organization in both emotional drain and lost opportunity? It happens everywhere, especially with fast-growth companies and the current economy's waves of layoffs and cuts. And I'm not even mentioning your personal life and what a lack of trust is costing you at home.

> "To be trusted is a greater compliment than to be loved."
> — George MacDonald

Trust is something that must be inspired, repaired, and maintained on an ongoing basis. I have seen trust erode before my very eyes and I have seen trust renewed as well. Do not believe it when people say trust cannot be restored — it can. It may never go back to what it was but, with forgiveness, it can go forward into something amazing and beautiful.

Patrick Lencioni says trust is all about vulnerability: "We must learn to be comfortable being open, even exposed to each other around our failures, weaknesses, even fears. People who refuse or are afraid to admit the truth about themselves will end up engaging in political behavior that wastes everyone's time and agenda."*

My friend, he is right on.

And as a leader, trust begins with you; the troops will follow. Trust begins with raising the level of trust you have in yourself. Then how much you allow yourself trust others. You go first!

When we have a lack of trust internally; we doubt and question, we waste time over analyzing. We waver in decision making, we beat ourselves up with negative self-talk, and we, of course then, cannot trust other people.

Developing self-trust leads to a new lease on life. When you have it, you are able to live with clarity!

When you trust yourself you can focus on what needs to be done and what can be left until tomorrow. When you live and honor your purpose and values, it becomes easier to discern when to say yes or no. This level of self-trust continues to feed upon itself and grow.

What step can you take to trust yourself and your team (even if that is your spouse) today?

* Patrick Lencioni, The Five Dysfunctions of a Team: A Leadership Fable (Jossey-Bass, 2002).

YOUR WEEKLY RESPONSE

What is my leadership intention this week? _____
_____
_____

How I will benefit from this shift? _____
_____
_____

What might hinder my success? _____
_____
_____

What action must I take in response? _____
_____
_____

What am I learning about myself? _____
_____
_____

What did I do this week that I am proud of? _____
_____
_____

WEEK 43: COMMUNICATION

AVOIDING THE BEACH BALL

IN BUSINESS, AS IN LIFE, THERE ARE MANY THINGS NOT IN YOUR control. Therefore, you must choose to impact everything that is in your sphere of influence with great care and purpose.

Whatever the challenge, prolonged uncertainty and concern and even battle fatigue can't be sustained. Leaders would be wise to clue in before it's too late.

Say you have staffers left behind after downsizing. The loss of colleagues has forced them to take on more responsibility outside their strength zone. When people adapt their behavior for a long period of time, stress gets to them. Usually it's not expressed verbally, or in any healthy, proactive way, but the pressure is mounting.

"People judge you by your actions, not your intentions. You may have a heart of gold, but so does a hard-boiled egg."

— Unknown Author

Think of holding a beach ball under the water. The action requires much effort and strength, and with just a minor slip, the ball shoots out of the water sideways, and maybe even hits an innocent bystander!

A wise leader will sense pressure amongst their team and create opportunity for relief. They find out what the people's strengths, talents, and skills are and organize the team accordingly. You would be surprised at what changing seats on the bus and getting people to have open communication will do, not only for the morale of the team but the good of the bottom line! You have so much wasted energy and talent on your team. The untapped potential in your people is costing you money. And most of all, it is burning out your star players.

Get ahead of the beach ball. Create an environment that attracts people (maybe those fleeing from a toxic culture, where the leader is more tyrannical). Invest in them. Encourage them. Learn what motivates them. Study what behavior style they manifest and then meet them where they are at and maximize it.

You can't control the market, but you control your culture, your time and energy investment, and your influence. You can impact your organization. You can be profitable and one of the best places to work. But it starts with you and your intentionality.

If you don't plan for it and budget for it now, you'll get whacked by that beach ball. Who on your team needs your investment of time, energy, and encouragement today?

YOUR WEEKLY RESPONSE

What is my leadership intention this week? _____
_____
_____

How I will benefit from this shift? _____
_____
_____

What might hinder my success? _____
_____
_____

What action must I take in response? _____
_____
_____

What am I learning about myself? _____
_____
_____

What did I do this week that I am proud of? _____
_____
_____

BUILDING A LEGACY NOW

DO YOU REALIZE THAT YOU HAVE AN INNATE DESIRE TO LIVE A LIFE that is significant, and leave a legacy that outlives you?

If you don't, then you may keep running on adrenaline, chasing the next thing — hoping it will bring you the satisfaction you are looking for and the answer to the question: How do I make a difference?

After selling PayPal for $1.5 billion, the 32-year-old co-founder, Max Levchin, still couldn't turn off his drive to succeed, and started a new company. I was fascinated when his fiancé got part of it right, telling a *New York Times* reporter on camera that it's not about the money for him, it's about the competition within him. However, Max himself diagnosed his own disease.

> "We're all destined to leave some kind of mark. We're all meant to walk a certain path at a certain time in a certain direction for a certain purpose."
>
> — Denzel Washington

Max: "On a grand scale I worry about being irrelevant. That is sorta my number one concern in life is I don't want to wake up and be in this sorta 'Where-Are-They-Now' file."

Most successful people are unconsciously trying to prove some-thing to someone. As we read in Week 11, it is a constant searching after the answer to the question, "Do I have what it takes?" and a desperate run from the fear, "What if I am found out?"

In short, we have a deep wound of insignificance: the feeling of having little or no meaning, value, or importance just as I am. The only way we feel worthy is when we keep producing, keep selling, keep moving — with the hope that one day we will achieve enough to stop having to prove ourselves to the unknown voice in our head. Mr. Levchin discovered that $1.5 billion isn't enough. What is?

I suggest that we start from the inside out. When we settle the issues inside of us, we usually accomplish so much more with so much less — and *also* give to our spouse, our kids, our neighbors, and the world.

Good for Max Levchin for speaking truth on what he is really after: a relevant, meaningful life. I wonder how long he will work 100 hours a week and how many companies he'll start before he realizes that relevance and significance are only found in what you do in the lives of others, meeting their needs — and many times those are intangible things without price tags.

YOUR WEEKLY RESPONSE

What is my leadership intention this week? _____
_____
_____

How I will benefit from this shift? _____
_____
_____

What might hinder my success? _____
_____
_____

What action must I take in response? _____
_____
_____

What am I learning about myself? _____
_____
_____

What did I do this week that I am proud of? _____
_____
_____

CHARACTER IN SMALL MOMENTS

I LOVE TO WATER-SKI! HOWEVER, EACH SUMMER I DREAD THE FIRST time out because I know I'll use muscles I forgot I had and will endure days of pain for my seven minutes of fun. Do I stop because it hurts? No, because I also know that those obscure muscles, if used, will soon be strengthened, and the pain will be replaced by being able to go faster, grab another buoy and have a blast on the water!

Right now you are undoubtedly facing one or more trials. The fight you had with your spouse, your aimless teenager, that dishonest employee, second-quarter financials, disgruntled shareholders — or perhaps all of the above: How you react and act to them is the measuring rod of where you truly stand in regard to your character.

"Too many people overvalue what they are not and undervalue what they are."
— Malcolm Forbes

Remember, "Character may be manifested in great moments, but it is made in small ones" (Phillip Brooks).

Okay, you probably realize that. But are you truly aware of whether or not you shortcut the amazing opportunities your trials are offering you? Do you shortcut your character development because it is too painful? Challenge yourself here, because in leadership, character is everything.

As Gen. H. Norman Schwarzkopf said, "Leadership is a combination of strategy and character. If you must be without one, be without the strategy."

So ask yourself, do you run away and work more hours or do you resolve the conflict at home? Do you buy your way out of guilt with gifts or actually resolve the problem with words? Do you have that difficult conversation with your worker, or do you hand if off to your direct report?

Character is gained during trials. Identifying areas of weakness is painful, but you have a choice to open your eyes, face the truth, realize you are not perfect, and become a better person. Or you can continue to avoid pain and live your guarded (and inevitably self-centered) life.

Enlarge your character by improving your weak side, and don't worry — after a few falls — you'll nail it. The reward will include the honor of being the person you have always greatly admired.

YOUR WEEKLY RESPONSE

What is my leadership intention this week? _____
_____
_____

How I will benefit from this shift? _____
_____
_____

What might hinder my success? _____
_____
_____

What action must I take in response? _____
_____
_____

What am I learning about myself? _____
_____
_____

What did I do this week that I am proud of? _____
_____
_____

WEEK 46: PURPOSE

LIVING THE ONLY DAY YOU HAVE

MEANING, PURPOSE, AND INTENTIONALITY. YOU PROBABLY KNOW THE logical reason why you do the things you do. But you may not know the *purpose* behind what you are logically doing day after day.

It is an important distinction. As leaders we have established plans, goals, and action steps that fit into our strategies. But we haven't taken time to figure out *why* what we do really matters.

Do you know deep in your heart that what you do, and who you are, really matters? To who? For what? And really — why?

> "If you don't have a vision, then your reality will always be determined by other's perceptions."
> — Melanee Addison

Think about it: If you only had one day to live, what would you do? What matters most? Well, today is the only day you know you have.

Relationships are the key. The truth is what you do for others is the only thing that truly matters in the end. Think about the times when life hit you hard and you were exposed financially or in another area where you required help. Suddenly you can't medicate the relationship pain / gap with money, busy living, and success. Look at your life. What do you find? The holes you try desperately to keep hidden are revealed in the spotlight.

So now is the time to exercise your choice. You can feel the emptiness, address the source, and discover your purpose. Or you can find a new way to numb yourself with more self-medicating than ever before. Medicating the gap is a protection we all use to some degree. If only we can come clean and admit it, we can be free to live our purpose.

Where are you getting your purpose, your joy, and your fulfillment? What is the name of the well you are drinking from right now? Every day you drop your bucket into a well — and up comes what? Remember, what you are drinking, you are becoming. Is your well toxic? Is it intoxicating? Is it refreshing? Is it stagnant? Is it full of you? What is in your well?

After you examine what well you are drinking from, then drink deeply — if it is the life-giving sustenance you are living for. If not, then let's dig a new well! Let's dig deep for what matters. Now is the time.

YOUR WEEKLY RESPONSE

What is my leadership intention this week? _____
_____
_____

How I will benefit from this shift? _____
_____
_____

What might hinder my success? _____
_____
_____

What action must I take in response? _____
_____
_____

What am I learning about myself? _____
_____
_____

What did I do this week that I am proud of? _____
_____
_____

PUSHING YOUR LIMITS

WHAT DO YOU THINK OF WHEN YOU HEAR SOMEONE (LIKE ME!) SAY, "You need to push your limits."

Envision yourself standing on a high peak of the Rocky Mountains watching a storm rage below. An eagle soars up through the thunderheads, and arcs toward the sun. The rainwater on his wings glistens like diamonds. Had it not been for the storm, the mighty raptor might have remained in the valley, and you wouldn't have caught a glimpse of its beauty.

Pushing through storms gives people the opportunity to grow in character, expand their sphere of influence, and live on higher ground. It strengthens our self-confidence and encourages us to keep reaching for more.

Being a coach, I push people every day to challenge their self-imposed limits and to go for the stretch goal. Faulty belief systems are the main thing that limits people in pursuing their personal greatness.

"Everyone thinks of changing the world, but no one thinks of changing himself."

— Leo Tolstoy

But the limits I see people breaking aren't the right ones. They are overloaded, and living on caffeine, adrenaline and mediocre success and yet they keep striving! Forgoing sleep, answering e-mails 24/7, working 60 hours a week, saying yes to every request, climbing the invisible ladder of success, justifying their adrenaline addiction. And then because they are overstretched, and calm themselves by eating, drinking, spending, or self-medicating.

We have confused which limits to break through and which ones to honor and create space for. What suffers is our true fulfillment and satisfaction with the things we do have, value, and desire in life. In fact, living a life of purpose, vision, and legacy is about moving beyond your own limits and comfort zone to something greater than you.

I invite you to decide where you need to set new limits for yourself to live intentionally by your values and to generate creative space for true living to occur.

YOUR WEEKLY RESPONSE

What is my leadership intention this week? _____
_____
_____

How I will benefit from this shift? _____
_____
_____

What might hinder my success? _____
_____
_____

What action must I take in response? _____
_____
_____

What am I learning about myself? _____
_____
_____

What did I do this week that I am proud of? _____
_____
_____

TRUST YOUR GUT

HERE'S THE SCENE: NEW WHITE RUNNING SHOES, PERFECTLY PLANNED walk with a dear friend, and a strict timeframe. The last part of the loop was a beautiful trail along Lake Washington albeit a bit swampy at times. Boy, I should have listened to my intuition.

As we started down the path, I got a bad feeling because there was mud on the trail. A few more steps and I thought, *Should we do this? We could still make it back in time if we turned around now.* I told myself I was just paranoid about getting my new shoes dirty. We made great progress until we came around a bend, and there was nothing but mud and I mean *mud.* We stopped dead in our tracks. We were too far in to go back. At the trail head, we had a choice. Now we were victims of that choice.

Our perfectly fun day turned into a stressful event because I didn't trust my gut.

> "It is not the brains that matter most, but that which guides them — the character, the heart, generous qualities, progressive ideas."
>
> — Fyodor Dostoevsky

In the working world there are more severe consequences of repeatedly ignoring your intuition than just stained shoes.

First, you can actually harden your heart to what you intuitively know is right. When you rationalize long enough, you dull yourself to the "check" in your gut. You also can distort your intuition so that you only hear what you want to hear. This causes you to make mistakes based on emotion. You fool yourself into feeling how you want to feel at the moment. Then the only way you can live with yourself is to rationalize your first decision until *you* are a muddy mess — what a vicious cycle.

How can you begin regaining the edge on your eroded intuition?

The best place to start sharpening your intuition is by working on your integrity.

My favorite definition of "integrity" is that your thoughts, words and actions are consistent and all in alignment. Usually the door leading you away from integrity is the same one you need to walk through to get back in. For example, if you knew you should have called your partner and told them about a mistake you made, but instead rationalized it away — go to them, apologize and make it right.

Listen to your gut; it has something to tell you!

YOUR WEEKLY RESPONSE

What is my leadership intention this week? _____
_____
_____

How I will benefit from this shift? _____
_____
_____

What might hinder my success? _____
_____
_____

What action must I take in response? _____
_____
_____

What am I learning about myself? _____
_____
_____

What did I do this week that I am proud of? _____
_____
_____

CHOOSING TO GO FORWARD

IF YOU'RE NOT FACING A BUSINESS CRISIS RIGHT NOW, YOU WILL BE soon. Are you prepared?

The waves are rough in a sea of adversity. But learning to swim in that setting provides you with one heck of an opportunity.

You may not be able to change the events and circumstances of the world around you. But you can choose your attitude, change your behavior, and act intentionally to take advantage of all the prospects that surround you.

However, until you stop reacting to the loss of "what was" and start responding to "what is," you will stay in an emotionally arrested state, hunkered down in a state of fear which will never produce the results you can be proud of.

> "We cannot change the past... We cannot change the fact that people will act a certain way. We cannot change the inevitable. The only thing we can do is play on the one string we have, and that is our attitude..."
>
> — Charles Swindoll

I am *not* saying, "Just think positive." What I am suggesting is, surround yourself with people who will tell you the truth and help you focus not on the "how" or the "what" of your operation, but on the "who" and "why."

What you can control, influence, and impact, do so. What you cannot control, surrender to. Not surrender in a give-up kinda way. Surrender in a courageous, bold way — intentionally dismissing the fear (false sense of controlling) and the negative self-limiting beliefs so that you may see through eyes of faith (the opposite of fear) to the amazing opportunities all around you.

Get help, get clear, and get in front of your team and talk to them! If you are scared and you actually have control, information, and power, consider your people's emotional state every waking hour of the day without control, information, or power. Pull your employees together and methodically process with them the emotion, the fear, and the uncertainty of what is going on. Get them on the same page of how to maximize results and creatively seize opportunities!

Once you have done that, look around your sphere of influence and help others do the same. People need the real you to lead them. Courage is key in a time like this. The faster you can come to grips with your own fears, the sooner you are ready to reignite hope and optimism from an authentic place.

YOUR WEEKLY RESPONSE

What is my leadership intention this week? _____
_____
_____

How I will benefit from this shift? _____
_____
_____

What might hinder my success? _____
_____
_____

What action must I take in response? _____
_____
_____

What am I learning about myself? _____
_____
_____

What did I do this week that I am proud of? _____
_____
_____

DISCOVERING THE WHY FACTOR

I WOULD LIKE YOU TO THINK FOR A MOMENT LIKE A GREAT COMPANY. We teach companies that their *why* (which we call purpose) must be discovered vs. made up. Your challenge is to discover what lies deep within you, correctly name it and then lead with it — this is your *why*. While *the what* is strategized and created, *the why* must be discovered and brought forth — in other words, it is already in there, so go get it.

When True Life Coaching celebrated ten years in business, we were proud to say that our *why* had not changed from day one. In contrast, our growth requires *the what* and *the how* to continuously evolve. Things never stay the same around here... except our *why*.

> "If you don't know where you are going, every road will get you nowhere."
>
> — Henry Kissinger

Currently on our roster are two companies in the fifth generation of ownership. Both are in the middle of a huge change of *the what* and *how*. What keeps them grounded is their unchanging *why*, which allows for agility as markets change and business models morph. It is super fun to watch new leadership continue their great-grandfathers' legacy.

At the same time, we are helping two start-ups who are growing spooky fast.

Company A is choosing to invest in the painstaking process of discovering their big *why*, defining their culture and strategy while differentiating themselves from the competition. The result is they are on track to make nearly 2X their projections, and doing it with fewer people, all who love their work!

Company B start-up unfortunately is still in the weeds. The leader is unwilling to take a moment to invest in *the why*, believing he can lead with his personality alone. The result is a bottom-line accomplishment of the *what* with a high emotional drain to other team players, not to mention the lost opportunities..

As a leader — whether of a company, a family or life — can you articulate what you are uniquely good at and why you are so excited about living your life? On that foundation, can you strengthen your *what* and *how* until you are not just good, but great?

Why does it matter? Why do you matter?

You matter because you have something distinctive and special to contribute to this world before you leave it. That's why.

YOUR WEEKLY RESPONSE

What is my leadership intention this week? _____
_____
_____

How I will benefit from this shift? _____
_____
_____

What might hinder my success? _____
_____
_____

What action must I take in response? _____
_____
_____

What am I learning about myself? _____
_____
_____

What did I do this week that I am proud of? _____
_____
_____

YOU CAN GO HIGHER

I REALLY DISLIKE IT (OKAY, I HATE IT) WHEN I AM CRUISIN' ALONG, accomplishing goals, thriving in relationships, and then all of a sudden something hits me out of the blue and completely throws off my game. A difficult person, negative, situation or perhaps even my own fear sucks my emotional energy and keeps me from going in the direction I need to go.

My creativity drops, my optimism is squelched, my heart feels heavy from not being sure how to get out of a funk. Sometimes roadblocks are healthy warning signs, but often they are ceilings that need to be pushed through and broken.

> *"Success is the ability to go from one failure to another with no loss of enthusiasm."*
> — *Winston Churchill*

This lesson popped out for me as I recently went paragliding off Tiger Mountain and hit the top of the thermal. I was begging my guide to take me higher so I could see more.

"We've hit a ceiling and so we're looking for a thermal disturbance so we can gain altitude," he said. He pointed out folks below in the same predicament. I watched as they found their entry point and bounced around a bit. But next thing I knew they were at eye level.

Then he said, "Okay, here we go!" The turbulence rocked us, but only for a moment, and we rode the thermal up to higher altitude. What a great view of the world!

It is the same experience for us as we try to gain ground at work or in life. Have you tried to go higher only to hit an invisible ceiling? Have you given up thinking you've hit your highest point, your top moment? It's a lie. You *can* go higher!

What bumpy air are you encountering? Do not confuse the sudden jerk as a setback. It may be exactly what is needed to prepare you for the adventure that lies ahead. When it is time to go to the next level, you must allow yourself to move out of your comfort zone and experience some turbulence.

Perspective and persistence are key to conquering self-imposed ceilings too. My paragliding instructor had to wait and search for the entry point out of our ceiling or we would have eventually descended.

What challenge are you facing that in fact might be a self-imposed ceiling?

YOUR WEEKLY RESPONSE

What is my leadership intention this week? _____
_____
_____

How I will benefit from this shift? _____
_____
_____

What might hinder my success? _____
_____
_____

What action must I take in response? _____
_____
_____

What am I learning about myself? _____
_____
_____

What did I do this week that I am proud of? _____
_____
_____

WHAT IS YOUR DREAM?

Forget the cliché question, "What is your passion?" There's a much more important one beyond it.

I was working with the CEO of Company X. Here's what I asked him. "Imagine that you have met all your financial goals and there are no obstacles in your way. What is your dream for Company X? What need would you like to see the profits and the people of this organization meet?"

What began to pour out of him was amazing — a vision much more inspiring and intriguing than the predictable statement framed in the lobby. I thought, *My gosh, if the people in his company knew* this *is what he was about — their potential would be unstoppable!*

That's the more important question: *What is your dream?*

"If you never have a dream, you'll never have a dream come true."
— Walt Disney

It is time to think beyond passion to your dream, because your dream determines your passion, your purpose, your motivation, and your very reason for existing

And the great news is, everyone has a dream. What is yours?

Before you start saying you want to "get married or have kids," or "retire to the sun," stop. I'm talking bigger.

What is unique about your dream is this: at its root a *need*. A need in others, to be exact. Your dream is a picture of a solution to a need that you are attracted to and would like to see met.

For example, I had a client who was a very successful marketing VP. He had trouble talking about a dream until I asked him, "What need, if it was met, would change the world?"

Instantly he said, "That all children would be literate." He had been a school teacher and loved it, but finances required him to be in the business world. We put in motion a step that he would start living his dream by tutoring one child one hour per week.

So now it's your turn to play. What are you really good at?

What do you truly enjoy doing?

What need do you see in the world you'd like to see met?

What is your big dream about that need?

Think about it. If everyone was living their dream, doing what they do best, and meeting the need they were specifically designed to meet... there would be no more need.

And you would find something you passionately wanted to do every day. No question about it.

YOUR WEEKLY RESPONSE

What is my leadership intention this week? _____
_____
_____

How I will benefit from this shift? _____
_____
_____

What might hinder my success? _____
_____
_____

What action must I take in response? _____
_____
_____

What am I learning about myself? _____
_____
_____

What did I do this week that I am proud of? _____
_____
_____

ABOUT SHANDEL SLATEN, MCC

As founder of True Life Coaching and its principal coach, Shandel Slaten helps entrepreneurs, executives, and employees of Fortune 500 firms become stronger leaders. A Master Certified Coach, she graduated summa cum laude with a degree in psychology, and holds certificates in Behavior Analysis, Professional Values Analysis, and Trimetrix HD.

A national speaker and author, Shandel has shared her wisdom via the "Ask Shandel" radio and podcast segment on a popular talk show. Shandel splits her time between Seattle and Reno, where she likes to spend time outdoors and loves being the favorite auntie to her nieces and nephews.

ABOUT TRUE LIFE COACHING

For over a decade, True Life Coaching has coached clients in skills that build trust, resolve conflict, and optimize business relationships.

True Life Coaching services and workshops offer customized, practical plans to get the results clients are looking for, whether it's a more productive working environment, improved communication, or a fresh approach to a challenging business partnership.

The coaches at True Life specialize in helping leaders operate with awareness and integrity so that they can develop high-performance teams that know their purpose. Leaders who invest in these plans are never disappointed with the ROI, and their teams reap rewards not only during the initial team-building exercises, but also in the long-term, bottom-line results.

Join in the conversation.
Find out more by visiting www.truelifecoaching.com.